LESSONS FROM JESUS

GREAT WORSHIP
FOR KIDS

Middler/Junior

STANDARD
PUBLISHING
Cincinnati, Ohio

Writers

Diana Crawford, Lessons 1-4
Vicki Ziese, Lessons 5-8
Peggy Schlieker, Lessons 9-13

Artists

Dina Sorn — 1A, 1C, 12B, 13A, 13B activity page art
Sherry F. Willbrand — all other activity page art

Scripture quotations marked *NIV* are from the HOLY BIBLE—NEW INTERNATIONAL VERSION, Copyright © 1973,1978, 1984 International Bible Society. Used by permission of Zondervan Bible Publishers.

Scriptures marked *ICB* quoted from the *International Children's Bible, New Century Version,* copyright © 1986, 1988 by Word Publishing, Dallas, Texas 75039. Used by permission.

The Standard Publishing Company, Cincinnati, Ohio
A division of Standex International Corporation
© 1993 by The Standard Publishing Company

ISBN 0-7847-0011-7

Table of Contents

It Doesn't Seem Great to Me . . .

What do you mean?

Great worship . . . Our Middler/Junior worship is hardly what you'd call great.

Why is that?

Well, I guess everyone has a different idea of what our worship time should be. Our Bible school superintendent calls it "extended session," and wants us to have a second Sunday school hour. But Sunday school is designed for instruction. Our worship time is for worshiping God.

That makes sense to me. What do the parents think?

Some of them want us to have a carbon copy of an adult worship service—including a sermon.

Uh-oh. That's not realistic for many Middlers and Juniors, is it?

In my experience it's not. Kids that age don't think like adults, respond like adults—and they certainly don't sit still as long as adults! I want them to worship God in ways that are appropriate for their level of development.

Absolutely. And you're not just keeping them occupied while their parents are in worship, as some people believe. The children's worship is as important and meaningful as the parents'.

Yes. I want every kid there to know God personally and to respond to Him in praise and thanksgiving. I want the kids to learn that worship is active, not passive. It's something they themselves do—not just the leader in front of the group.

Sounds to me as if you're right on target. What makes your Middler/Junior worship less than great?

It's hard to involve all the pupils sometimes. There are older kids and younger kids. Some are quick and bright, and some work more slowly and need more encouragement. Some are more comfortable in small groups than others. It's hard to appeal to all their differences.

The writers of *Great Worship for Kids* know that's true. They've tried to consider individual differences as they've planned worship sessions. As you examine each session you'll find some activities that are easy, some that are more difficult. Some appeal to pupils who like to research or to work puzzles, and some to pupils who like to speak and act. Each session will have something that addresses the needs of each pupil.

I guess so. And even if a pupil doesn't get into the activities one week, the following week he can find something he likes. But while we're talking about the number of activities in each session, what about the number of adult leaders needed for all the small groups? There are only two of us, and we can't be everywhere!

One solution is to use a cassette recorder. Tape record instructions for one or more of the small groups and have those groups work independently. Or photocopy the instructions for pupils to read. Ask an older or more mature pupil to serve as "chairperson" of the group to keep things moving.

I've tried that. As a matter of fact, during the week before the session I contact pupils to be chairpersons. That way I can give them special instructions so they'll be prepared. And it's good to get to know the pupils better and make them feel special.

Great! And then during *Building the Theme* you can circulate between groups as they need attention. You can also choose only one or two activities to prepare in small groups, and do the rest of the session as a large group. And—though it's not ideal—you can always omit parts of *Sharing in Worship* if they can't be prepared in small groups.

I always hate to leave things out. But actually, I feel as though we get into a rut sometimes anyway, so I guess it's not so bad to drop something from time to time. We do many of the same things every week. Take music, for instance. The kids either write words for a song, sing songs, or choose songs for the group to sing. It's so predictable!

So is adult worship. Think about what is done in most churches today—the same things, often in the same order,

Sunday after Sunday. Your Middlers and Juniors may not find it objectionable to do the same things over and over—they may find security in activities that are familiar to them.

I wish *I* felt more secure . . . about how to split up the pupils into small groups, I mean. The rowdy kids want to be in a group together, and then they end up wasting time and cutting up. And the shy kids just sit and look at each other for half their group time before they can get started working together. Any suggestions?

As leader you can always assign groups yourself, mixing the groups as you choose. Whenever you possibly can, however, allow the pupils to volunteer for groups they're interested in. The easiest way to do this is to have sign-up sheets. Indicate on each sheet the maximum number of pupils who may sign up so you don't have nine kids working a crossword puzzle while only two prepare to act out a Bible story. You can always choose groups at random, also—having the pupils draw numbers out of a hat or count off. The key is to vary things as much as you can, but always to do what works best with your kids in your group.

And you know, the kids I lead are . . . well, they're just great kids. I love them all.

What was that—about the kids, I mean?

I love them.

No, what you said before that.

They're great kids.

And when they worship?

What? Oh, I get it! Great kids—GREAT WORSHIP!

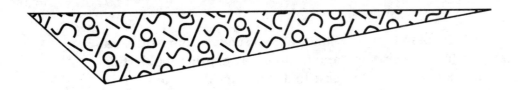

If You've Never Used Great Worship for Kids,

here are some things you need to know:

This book contains 13 sessions. The sessions are based on Scriptures and lessons from Standard Publishing's Middler and Junior Sunday school curriculum.

Each worship session is planned so that pupils work in small groups to prepare the elements of the worship time (call to worship, Scripture, special music, devotion, offering, Lord's Supper, prayer, or personal praise). The elements the small groups have prepared are then incorporated into the worship time.

Each weekly session is designed to last 80-95 minutes. It begins with *Transition Time,* a flexible time between Sunday school and Middler/Junior worship. This is a casual time for relaxation and conversation. It includes a rest room and drink break, as well as a game or activity that allows the children to move around. This freedom is important after the pupils have been sitting during the Sunday school hour.

Involving the children in organized activity as soon as they arrive avoids confusion and eliminates the moments you spend gathering children from the halls when you are ready to begin the worship time.

During *Launching the Theme,* the leader introduces the theme of the session to the children. This is done through a story, object lesson, or dialogue. Involving pupils during this section is a priority. The leader also explains the small group choices and guides the pupils in choosing the groups they are interested in.

Building the Theme is the time when pupils work in their groups to prepare the elements of the worship time. Adult leaders work with the small groups to help them stay on track. Then during *Sharing in Worship* the large group gathers for worship time. An adult leader directs this time and integrates the small group activities so the pupils participate in worship.

Closing Moments is the flexible time between the end of Middler/Junior worship and the end of adult worship. This section lists a variety of activities, but each one can be dropped quickly and easily when the adult service is over.

Activity pages are included with each session plan. You are free to photocopy any of the pages for use with your worship group, but you are NOT permitted to photocopy any of the music that appears in this book. To do so is a violation of copyright.

Worship Plan Sheet

Session _____   Date _____

Unit Title_____

Session Title _____

Scripture Text_____

Worship Focus_____

Transition Time   Leader _____

Materials: _____

_____

Preparation: _____

_____

Procedure: _____

_____

_____

_____

Launching the Theme   Leader _____

Materials: _____

_____

Preparation: _____

_____

Procedure: _____

_____

_____

_____

Building the Theme

Group 1. _____   Leader _____

Materials: _____

_____

Preparation: _____

_____

Procedure: _____

_____

_____

Group 2. _____   Leader _____

Materials: _____

_____

Preparation: _____

_____

Procedure: _____

_____

Group 3. _____   Leader _____

Materials: _____

_____

Preparation: _____

_____

Procedure: _____
_____
_____

Group 4. _____   Leader _____
Materials: _____

Preparation: _____

Procedure: _____
_____
_____

Group 5. _____   Leader _____
Materials: _____

Preparation: _____

Procedure: _____
_____
_____

Group 6. _____   Leader _____
Materials: _____

Preparation: _____

Procedure: _____
_____
_____

Sharing in Worship   Leader _____
_____
_____
_____
_____
_____
_____
_____
_____
_____

Closing Moments   Leader _____
Materials: _____

Preparation: _____

Procedure: _____
_____
_____

Jesus Had Power From God

Worship Focus

Worship God because He is powerful.

Transition Time

(10-15 minutes)

Send pupils to the rest room and water fountains. As other pupils arrive, make sure all are involved in the following activity.

Beforehand write some medical terms on small pieces of paper. Place the papers in a container. In class the pupils can use these terms to play an adaptation of "Charades."

To play, one person draws out a word and acts out that word without speaking. If a person guesses correctly, he or she becomes the next actor.

Use the following terms: doctor, nurse, medicine, stethoscope, sickness, fever, thermometer, shot. You may want to add other medical terms to this list.

Launching the Theme

(10 minutes)

You'll need to provide a dictionary for this activity. You'll also need poster board or a chalkboard on which the pupils can list their brainstorm ideas. Assign one small group to look up the meaning of the word *power* in the dictionary and write down the various definitions.

The rest of the group should be brainstorming ideas about people or items they think have power or are powerful. Suggestions might include the president of the United States, a boss, a rich person who has power, a strong medicine, thunder and lightning, or a magnet.

After you have the group read the definitions and discuss their ideas, make sure you stress the following:

We think of many things when we think of the word *power*. But no powerful person or thing can compare with God's power. God gave Jesus the power to heal sickness and raise people from the dead. We come together today to worship a powerful God—a God who has the power to help us deal with any problems we could have.

Building the Theme

• • • • • • • • • • • • • • • • •

(30 minutes)

1. Call to Worship. Pupils will write and prepare to deliver a choral reading based on James 5:13-16. Provide Bibles, copies of activity page 1A and pencils or pens.

Have the pupils look at activity page 1A. Beside each phrase of the Bible verse are lines for pupils to write phrases to expand on the Scripture. They should complete the entire page.

Once the group has finished writing, have the group decide on parts and practice reading what they have written. Use the reading instructions given on the page.

These pupils will present the Call to Worship during *Sharing in Worship.*

2. Scripture. Pupils will research Scriptures that describe God's power and will prepare a visual demonstration.

Provide Bibles, paper, pencils, markers.

Jesus' power to help and heal is shown many times in the Bible. We call these events miracles. Let's investigate some of these now. Use the following references: Luke 4:38-40; Luke 5:17-26; Matthew 17:14-21; John 9:1-34; Luke 13:10-17; and Luke 17:11-19. Pupils can read each reference and answer the following questions: Whom did Jesus heal in these verses? What was the problem or illness in each case? How did Jesus help?

Assign one reference to each pupil in the group. The pupil should draw a symbol of power on his sheet, write the reference on the sheet, and be able to tell some information about the miracle.

This group will present the Scripture.

3. Special Music. Pupils will practice and present the song, "Power."

Provide Bibles, pencils, crayons, markers, and drawing paper. You may also want to record the song on cassette tape so the pupils may practice. Or have someone play an instrument to help pupils learn the song.

To prepare for worship today, we first want to read about some instances in which Jesus used His power from God to heal people. (Use the Scripture references listed in the second activity.) Ask individuals to look up the Scripture references and report to the group.

Have the words for this song printed on a poster or on the overhead projector. Practice the song with the pupils several times. If desired, ask certain pupils to sing individual verses as solos.

If you have the time, you might want to have pupils draw pictures to illustrate the Scripture references. Or create another verse to the song using one of the other Scripture references.

During *Sharing in Worship,* the pupils will sing and teach the song to the group.

POWER
(Tune: "BINGO")

Jesus had power to raise the dead.
He raised Jairus' daughter.
P-o-w-e-r, p-o-w-e-r, p-o-w-e-r.
We praise You, Jesus, for Your pow'r.

Jesus had power to heal the sick.
He healed the crippled woman.
P-o-w-e-r, p-o-w-e-r, p-o-w-e-r.
We praise You, Jesus, for Your pow'r.

Jesus had power to give men sight.
He healed the man born blind.
P-o-w-e-r, p-o-w-e-r, p-o-w-e-r.
We praise You, Jesus, for Your pow'r.

Jesus had power to make men well.
He healed the crippled lepers.
P-o-w-e-r, p-o-w-e-r, p-o-w-e-r.
We praise You, Jesus, for Your pow'r.

4. Life-Size Get-Well Card. Pupils will research Scriptures about God's care and will design a life-size get-well card that will be shown during the offering time and later given to someone in the congregation.

Obtain mural paper, markers, Bibles, pencils, scissors. Have one pupil lie on the paper while you trace around him or her. Have another pupil cut on the lines.

Assign one Scripture to each pupil in this group. The pupil is to find the Scripture and read it, then copy it on the body part that is mentioned in the references. Pupils should decide how God's care is shown in each verse and write this along with the verse. Pupils may decide to decorate the card to look like a real person.

Use the following Scriptures. The words in parentheses are to help you determine the significance of the verses for today's lesson. Use them only if pupils cannot come up with their own ideas.

Head—Psalm 23:5 (God is powerful enough to provide all our needs, even in difficult situations.)

Hands—Isaiah 49:16 (God will never forget us.)

Arms—Deuteronomy 33:27 (God will always be there to care for us.)

Heart—Psalm 37:4 (God has the power to give you anything.)

Feet—Psalm 66:9 (God will keep us from making mistakes, if we trust Him.)

Body—1 Corinthians 6:19, 20; Philippians 1:20 (We are precious in God's sight. He sent Jesus to be our Savior.)

5. Power Plays. Pupils will work to resolve some situations in which boys and girls have to depend on God's power. Provide copies of page 1B, pencils, Bibles.

Do you realize that our very powerful God can help you with any problems you have? Sometimes we try to work out problems on our own, but we're not very successful. Let's look at some situations where boys and girls your age are having to make some similar decisions.

Distribute activity page 1B. Assign one pupil to do each situation or discuss them all together as a group. Give the group time to work independently before you discuss solutions. While their opinions may differ on ways to handle a situation, make sure they base their answers on Biblical principles.

During *Sharing in Worship,* members of the group will read the situations, discuss their answers, and tell why they think that way.

6. Power Prayers. Pupils will read and present a personal prayer they composed using Scriptures about God's power.

Provide copies of activity page 1C, pencils, and Bibles.

Because our powerful God is listening to our prayers, we can ask Him for help in dealing with our lives. And after we ask God for help, we need to act on our request.

As you look up these Scripture passages, think about how you will ask God to help you.

Ask good readers to read the Scripture passages aloud. Then read the statements on the activity page and have pupils fill in the statements for themselves. Make suggestions as needed for ways the pupils can act on the passages listed.

Then help the pupils decide how they want to read the prayer aloud. They will present this prayer during the prayer time of *Sharing in Worship.*

Sharing in Worship
● ● ● ● ● ● ● ● ● ● ● ● ● ● ●
(20-25 minutes)

Omit any of the following sections if you did not offer the corresponding activity.

Call to Worship (Group 1): At this time we worship God because He gave Jesus the power to heal and do miracles.

Think about this while Group 1 presents our call to worship. Group 1 will read their choral reading at this time.

Music: Let's worship our God by singing several praise and worship songs. Suggestions could include several stanzas of "God Is So Good" (God is so powerful . . . He can raise the dead, etc.).

Scripture (Group 2): **Group 2 has researched Scriptures about Jesus' power. The pupils will hold up their papers, with symbols of power, and explain their Scripture passages.**

Special Music (Group 3): **Group 3 will teach you a song about Jesus' power.** Group 3 will sing the song through first. Then sing the song together as a group. Either use the tape recording or have someone play the melody on the piano.

Lord's Supper: Jesus loved us so much that He died on the cross for our sins. (Read 1 Corinthians 6:14.) But we do not remember a dead hero. God used His incredible power to raise Jesus from the dead. Let's take time to think about how much our powerful God loves us.

Offering (Group 4): **In response to God's power and His love for us, we give our money and we help others. Group 4 made a large get-well card that they will share and explain at this time.**

Ask pupils to collect the offering while the group is showing their card. The group will need to decide to whom they want to give the card.

Devotion (Group 5): Group 5 presents their power plays at this time. After each is presented, allow time for discussion on whether or not God's power was displayed in this person's life.

Today, we've talked about the power of God. But you can see from these role plays, if you do not ask for God's help and His power, your life as a Christian will not be strong.

The most important thing is to talk to God and ask for His help. You can't handle all of life's problems by yourself.

Another thing to do is to memorize one of the Scriptures mentioned today about power. Then, if you get in a difficult situation, you'll be able to recall that verse to give you strength.

If God could bring a child back from the dead, He can help you with problems at school or with your family or your friends. He can give you the strength to speak up when you need to, or help someone, even when it is very difficult.

As Group 6 reads their power Scriptures, listen carefully. Try to decide which one of these verses means the most to you and think about it at this time.

Prayer (Group 6): Group 6 will present their reading of the prayer they composed.

Closing Moments
● ● ● ● ● ● ● ● ● ● ● ● ● ●
(10-15 minutes)

Have the rest of the group sign personal messages on the life-size get-well card.

Provide index cards and pencils. Have each pupil choose one of the Scriptures listed by Group 6 and copy it on the card. Encourage the pupils to use their cards as a beginning to a braver time this week.

PRESCRIPTION: PRAYER

Use James 5:13-16 to fill in the blanks.

Is anyone in trouble? He should _____.
Is anyone happy? He should _____.
Is anyone sick? He should _____
_____.

Now fill in the blanks with ideas of your own.

Is anyone lonely? He should _____.
Is anyone hurting? He should _____.
Is anyone sad? He should _____.
Is anyone rich? He should _____
_____.

"Therefore _____ your sins to _____
_____ and _____ for each other so that you
may be _____. The _____
of a _____ man is powerful
and effective."

James 5:16

Power Plays

Read these situations and decide how the boys and girls involved need God's power in their lives.

Allen's parents are getting a divorce. Allen's angry all the time. He's started fighting with his friends, and sometimes he feels like running away from home. How can Allen use God's power?

Shakeisha's favorite aunt is very ill in the hospital. Shakeisha is close to her aunt, so she is very upset. She's having trouble sleeping and her grades have fallen. How can Shakeisha use God's power?

Ashley's Sunday school class has been learning about witnessing to others. Her teacher has encouraged the class members to choose someone to invite to a party they're having at the church. Ashley is shy, and when she thinks about speaking up, she feels kind of sick to her stomach. How can Ashley use God's power?

Now list some areas in your own life in which you know you need God's power.

1. _____

2. _____

3. _____

Choose one area to work on this week.

Power Prayer

Use these Scriptures to remind you of God's power in your life.
Read through all of them, and then use one of the verses to write your own prayer.

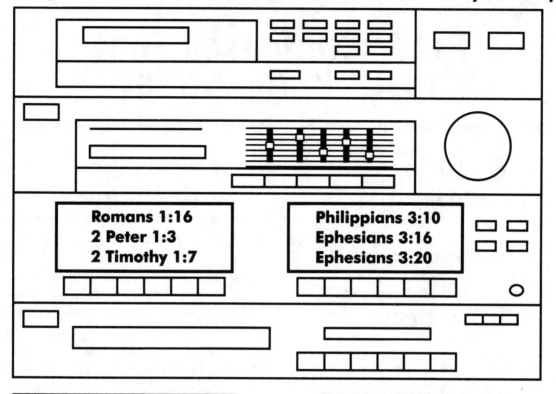

Romans 1:16
2 Peter 1:3
2 Timothy 1:7

Philippians 3:10
Ephesians 3:16
Ephesians 3:20

Here is an example:

Since You did not give us a spirit of fear, but a spirit of power, of love, and self-discipline (2 Timothy 1:7), I don't have to be afraid to speak up about You. Help me to talk to Shavon and invite him to come to church with me.

Now you write one:

Since _____

_____

_____

_____

(_____)

I will not be afraid. I will _____

_____

_____

_____ .

Peter Confesses That Jesus Is the Christ

Worship Focus

• • • • • • • • • • • • • • • •

Worship God by confessing His Son Jesus to be the Christ.

Transition Time

• • • • • • • • • • • • • • • •

(10-15 minutes)

Take a break and send pupils to the rest room and water fountain. Involve newcomers and other pupils in the following activity.

Beforehand write each word of the memory verses, Acts 2:22, 36, on a separate index card or piece of paper. (If possible, use the ICB version of the Bible.) Then while the pupils are gone on break, hide the pieces of paper throughout the room. When pupils enter the room, they are to look for the slips of paper, and then put them in order to read the memory verses. After the verses are read, see if pupils can say the verses again without looking at the papers.

Launching the Theme

• • • • • • • • • • • • • • • •

(10 minutes)

Before class, obtain some of the following: copies of the wedding ceremony and vows, copies of the Girl Scout and Boy Scout promises, copies of other vows or contracts.

Have you ever been to a wedding ceremony? The two people getting married make a vow or promise to each other that they will love and be devoted to that person only. They make their vows in front of witnesses. (You may want to read the vows aloud.)

When you become a Christian you make a statement about who Jesus is and what He means to you. You make this statement in front of witnesses too.

That's why we're looking at the "Good Confession" that Peter made. It's not like confessing something you did was right or wrong—but stating in front of people what Jesus really means to you. Another way of stating this is saying you "confess Christ." There are many ways to confess Christ in your life by what you do and what you say. We will show our belief in Him today by worshiping Him.

Building the Theme

• • • • • • • • • • • • • • •

(30 minutes)

Select from these activities to meet the needs of your learners. Some aspects of worship can be a part of *Sharing in Worship* even though there's not a related activity.

1. Call to Worship. Pupils will create a rebus of Romans 10:8-10 to introduce the worship service.

Provide Bibles, shelf or butcher paper, markers and crayons, pencils, masking tape to attach the mural to the wall. (You may want to have the sheet hanging on the wall before pupils come.)

Romans 10:8-10 talks about how we "confess" Christ with our mouths and our hearts. We're going to illustrate these three verses as a rebus mural. Let's read through these verses now. Make sure all pupils find the verses. As a pupil reads the verses aloud, the group should be thinking about which words can be substituted with drawings (heart, mouth, Jesus, word, etc.).

The pupils will print the words of the verses, but leave space to draw pictures for the designated words. Divide the verses so small groups can work on each verse.

When the mural is completed, practice reading the three verses aloud.

During *Sharing in Worship*, the pupils will display and read the rebus as the Call to Worship.

2. Special Music. These pupils will prepare to lead worship songs. Provide the music and words for songs related to confessing Christ's name. If you can, provide a cassette tape on which you've recorded the songs so pupils can practice. Or have someone who plays an instrument available to help the pupils

practice. You may want to provide song charts or overhead transparencies if any of these songs is new to your pupils.

Following are some songs that would be appropriate: "Jesus, Jesus, Lord to Me," "His Name Is Wonderful," "All Hail King Jesus," and "Praise the Name of Jesus."

Read through the words of the songs and talk about any terms your pupils might not understand. If a song is new to the entire group, decide how the group will teach the song during worship.

3. Scripture Search. Pupils will research Scriptures to discover how we confess Christ in the things we do in our worship. You'll need to make sure that pupils understand confessing Christ isn't just saying the words. We show our belief in and respect for Him by all the things we say and do.

Provide Bibles, copies of activity page 2A, pencils, copies of your own church bulletin.

There are several verses in the Bible that help explain why we do various things in worship. Just as Peter stated who Jesus is, we show who Jesus is by the things we say and do during our worship. Let's look at some of the verses now.

You can either have the whole group look up each verse together or divide the verses so a few pupils look up each one and read it aloud to the group. Go through each verse, discuss it, and compare it to what is listed in the pupil worship or adult worship.

Each part of our worship confesses Christ. We praise God with our songs and words in worship. Our prayers acknowledge Jesus as God's Son. We pray in His name because we believe in His power. By expressing our love and fellowship toward one another we show the world that we belong to Jesus. Every sermon that is preached will ultimately acknowledge God's power and Jesus as His Son.

The Communion service is the most special time where we can confess Christ and show our love for Him. The same is true of the offering. Our giving shows our love and loyalty to God's Word and His work.

At the end of the service, people can come forward to be baptized. This is the most exciting and visible way that a person confesses Christ.

To present this part of *Sharing in Worship,* assign each part of the service to a pupil. During worship, the pupil can share his verses and tell why or how this part confesses Christ.

4. The Name Game. There are many titles and names for Jesus. Pupils will compile a list of names and titles from the Bible that refer to Jesus and who He is.

Provide Bibles, concordances, paper and pencils, chart paper.

With an adult's help, pupils can research through the concordance to find as many names as possible for Jesus. They should make a list of these names on the chart paper.

During *Sharing in Worship,* the pupils will present their information to set the tone for the Communion time.

5. Devotion. Pupils will investigate Bible people who confessed Jesus and/or told others who He was.

Provide Bibles, copies of activity page 2B, pencils.

The activity is written in the form of riddles. See if pupils can identify the people without looking up the Scripture references.

There are times mentioned in the Bible where people confessed Christ or told others who He was. We're going to look at some of these people now.

Read through each passage separately. See if you can guess who the person is from the riddle. As you're reading, ask yourself, "What does this person think about Jesus? Who does he or she say

Parts of Worship

Read each Scripture reference to discover different parts of worship. In the third column, make notes about how we worship today.

Scripture	Aspect of worship mentioned	How we worship today
Colossians 3:16, 17		
1 John 3:22		
Matthew 18:20		
1 Corinthians 1:23, 24		
Acts 4:33-35		
1 Corinthians 11:23-26		
Galatians 3:26, 27		

Activity Page 2A

Jesus really is?" Use the Scriptures if pupils can't guess the riddles.

To present during *Sharing in Worship,* each pupil can read aloud one riddle and ask the group to guess who the person is.

6. Sing-a-Prayer. Pupils in this group will lead the prayer time by singing the song, "Father, I Adore You." Ask these pupils to write new verses to the song. Provide Bibles and concordances, along with paper and pencils, so pupils can use various titles and names for Jesus in their verses. If pupils find this difficult, use the two verses below as examples.

> Father, I confess you.
> Tell each person I love you.
> I will speak for you.
>
> Son of God, I love you.
> I'll tell others about you.
> I will speak for you.

After the group has written their new verses, they should copy the words on a large song chart or chalkboard so all pupils can see the words. They will need to decide if they are going to sing the words as a group, or as individuals. They also need to decide which verses to teach the large group so they also can sing their worship.

Sharing in Worship
(20-25 minutes)

Omit any of the following sections if you did not offer the corresponding activity.

Call to Worship (Group 1): **We worship God when we confess Him, or tell others about what He means to us. Let's worship Jesus now and tell Him how special He is to us.** Group 1 holds up their rebus mural and reads Romans 10:8-10.

Music (Group 2): **Many songs are written about the name of Jesus. When we think about Jesus we can think about all the names and titles He has. Let's worship God by singing about His Son, Jesus.**

Lord's Supper (Group 4): **Peter stated that Jesus is the Christ, the Son of God. Jesus is the only one who ever died and came back to life by His own power. God is the only one who could give Jesus that kind of power. Group 4 has made a list of names and titles for Jesus. During your quiet prayer time, think about these names and thank God for His gift of Jesus.** Group 4 should read their list at this time.

Offering: We confess Jesus or show our love for Him when we give our money. Ask two pupils to collect the offering.

Devotion (Group 5): **Group 5 has some riddles they will read to you. See if you can guess who these people are who confess Christ.** (Pupils can take turns reading the riddles aloud and having the large group guess.)

I have a question for you! How can you confess Christ each day? (We confess Christ by our actions when we act the way He acted when He lived on earth.) **What are some things you could do each day to act Christ-like?** (Allow responses.) **We can confess Christ by obeying our parents, teachers, and God. We can confess Christ by loving and helping others. We can confess Christ by keeping our thoughts, words, and actions as pure as possible. We confess Christ when we take a stand for Him.**

It's not easy to confess Christ with our lives every day. It's much harder than just saying some words. It's even harder to tell people why our actions differ from those of many others. But look how Peter was blessed by Jesus. We will ultimately be blessed too.

Scripture (Group 3): **This group has researched activities that confess Christ. They will explain why we worship the way we do.**

Let each member of this group tell about one aspect of worship and how it confesses Christ.

Prayer (Group 6): **Let's close our worship today by singing our prayers to Jesus. Group 6 will lead us.** Group 6 will teach the new verses to the large group and everyone sings the prayer song.

Closing Moments
(10-15 minutes)

Hand out activity page 2C and pencils. Pupils should prayerfully consider how they will confess Christ in their thoughts, words, and actions this week as they fill out the page. Have a closing prayer asking God for help so the pupils will be able to confess Christ.

Parts of Worship

Read each Scripture reference to discover different parts of worship.
In the third column, make notes about how we worship today.

Scripture	Aspect of worship mentioned	How we worship today
Colossians 3:16, 17		
1 John 3:22		
Matthew 18:20		
1 Corinthians 1:23, 24		
Acts 4:33-35		
1 Corinthians 11:23-26		
Galatians 3:26, 27		

Riddle This

Read these clues to discover people who confessed Jesus as the Christ.
If you can't identify the person from the clue alone, read the Scripture.

John 3:1, 2

I was a member of the Pharisees who wanted to talk to Jesus.

Luke 4:33-35

I told who Jesus was, even though I was not myself at the time.

Luke 19:1-8

I had to meet Jesus from the branch of a tree, but I found out who He really is.

Luke 17:12-14

We were very sick with a terrible disease, but we knew who Jesus was.

Luke 18:35-43

I knew who Jesus was, but everyone told me to be quiet!

Luke 23:44-47

I saw the weather change, and I knew about Jesus.

John 4:29, 39-42

Thirst helped me to find out who Jesus is.

John 11:25-27

When my brother died, I discovered who Jesus is.

John 20:26-28

I wanted a "hands-on" experience before I would believe who Jesus is.

All of Me

Be creative! Think of different ways you can confess Christ throughout the day.

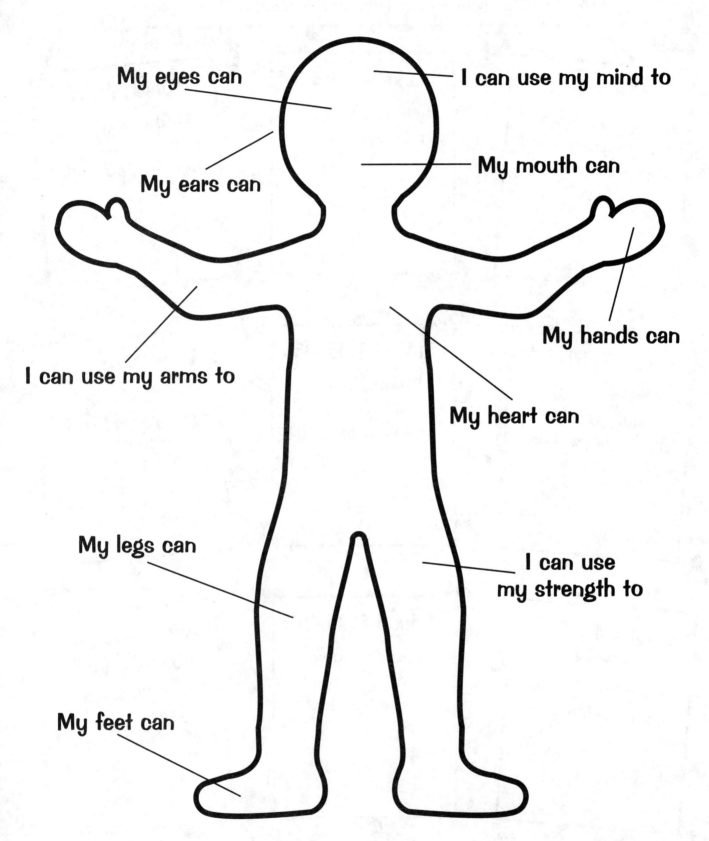

My eyes can

I can use my mind to

My ears can

My mouth can

I can use my arms to

My hands can

My heart can

My legs can

I can use my strength to

My feet can

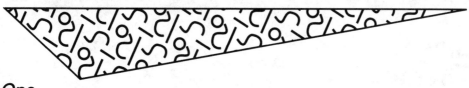

God Says Jesus Is His Son

Worship Focus

Worship God by glorifying His Son, Jesus.

Transition Time

(10-15 minutes)

Send pupils to the rest room and water fountain. Involve all newcomers and other pupils in this following activity. If you have more pupils than this, duplicate names. Explain that these are all names or titles for Jesus.

Write the following terms on pieces of paper:

King	Light of the World	Teacher
Life	Living Water	Jehovah
Jesus	Bread of Life	Savior
Lord	Good Shepherd	Emmanuel
Truth	Lamb of God	Son of God

Attach one slip of paper to the back of each pupil. Pupils must ask each other questions in order to guess their names. They can ask only yes-or-no questions. After a period of time, if they have not guessed, they can ask other questions. Then let each pupil tell his name or title.

Launching the Theme

(10 minutes)

Bring in copies of items that are considered recommendations, such as a resume, a movie critic's column, a college application that calls for references, etc.

If you want to find out about a certain movie or restaurant, you can read critics' recommendations. When you fill out an application for a job or for college, you usually need to have references. These references are written by people who will speak up for you, and will say good things about you. Because you pick trustworthy people to be references, their recommendations can be believed.

Jesus had the greatest reference anyone could have—God himself. God made sure that the disciples knew Jesus really is His Son by telling them himself. Because God is trustworthy and always keeps His word, we can believe what He says about His Son, Jesus. Today we worship God and His Son, Jesus. We'll see how God told people that Jesus is His Son. Then we will worship God by glorifying His Son, Jesus.

Building the Theme

• • • • • • • • • • • • • • • •

(30 minutes)

1. Call to Worship: Provide tools (pencils, paper, Bible dictionaries, regular dictionary, topical Bible or chain reference Bible) so pupils can look up the definition of the word *glory.* Ask them to use the dictionaries and list ways they can give glory to Jesus.

Sometimes God's glory was shown in a dramatic or physical way such as at the Transfiguration. Other times "glory" means a characteristic of God or Jesus we can't see, such as holiness or wisdom.

In many places the Bible talks about our "glorifying" Jesus. These instances may include praise, exalt, show respect for, obey, put first, give credit to, please, honor, revere, love, say good things about, worship.

Today we are going to worship God by glorifying His Son, Jesus, by the things we do and say.

Ask pupils in this group to list the definitions of "glory" on a large sheet of paper or the chalkboard so the whole group can see them. You may want to ask each pupil in the group to draw a picture to illustrate one definition. Then the pupils can show their illustrations during the Call to Worship portion of *Sharing in Worship.*

2. Scripture Diary. Pupils in this group compose a diary entry reporting the emotions felt by the three disciples during the Transfiguration.

Pupils will need Bibles, pencils, and activity page 3A. Read the instructions and make sure pupils understand the activity. Depending on your group, you may want each pupil to write his or her own diary entry or write one diary entry together as a group.

Dear Diary

Try to put yourself in place of the apostles present at the Transfiguration. How do you think you might have felt or reacted to all that happened? Write a diary entry as you think one of the apostles might have written.

Dear Diary,
I can't believe what has happened . . . but I saw it with my own eyes.
_____
_____
_____
_____
_____
_____

What will happen to me next as I work and learn from Jesus?
Signed,

Activity Page 3A

To get pupils started, discuss the emotions and ideas the disciples had while the Transfiguration was going on. The disciples might have been alarmed or frightened, or they might have felt honored that they were a part of this event.

After your discussion, allow pupils some time to work. Give help as needed.

These pupils will present their diary entries during the Scripture portion of *Sharing in Worship.*

3. Special Music. Pupils will sing an adaptation of the song, "Bless the Lord, O My Soul," and present an acrostic. Before class, you may want to write the words either on an overhead transparency or on a piece of poster board so the pupils can practice. You'll need to decide whether you want to use a taped accompaniment or an instrument. You'll also need markers, paper, pencils, a large piece of poster board, and Bibles to make the acrostic.

To begin, write the names *Jesus Christ* vertically on the chalkboard. Ask pupils to think of character traits about Jesus, or things Jesus does for us, that begin with the letters in His name.

Some examples might include:

J—joyous
E—eternal, encourager
S—supportive
U—understanding, etc.

Pupils may think of other words and phrases. Assign one letter to each child to think of a word and then illustrate it. You may want to make giant letters, and have pupils write the words and illustrations inside the letters.

After they do this, work on the extra verses to the song, "Bless the Lord, O My Soul." Here are some possible words. Pupils can come up with others on their own.

He has done great things;
He has done great things;
He has done great things.
Bless His Holy name.

Have the pupils try to think of verses using the words from the acrostic. For example, "He is understanding," or, "He encourages me."

These pupils will present their acrostic and special music during *Sharing in Worship.*

4. Music. Pupils will look through hymnals and songbooks for songs about praise and glorifying Jesus.

Provide hymnals and songbooks, paper, pencils, and blank transparencies and transparency pens. Encourage the pupils to look for at least three songs on those two themes.

Pupils can either sing the songs for the large group or lead the group in singing or reading the words as a choral reading. If all the group is to be singing, have pupils write the words on the overhead transparencies. They'll need to decide who sings or speaks which songs. While they're working, encourage pupils to look for what the songs say about praising or glorifying Jesus. Pupils will lead the song service during *Sharing in Worship.*

5. Devotion. Pupils will design praise posters to show during the devotion portion of *Sharing in Worship.*

Begin by putting this sentence on the chalkboard or on a piece of poster board: "I can give glory to Jesus by . . . "

Ask the group to think about ideas on how they can glorify Jesus. Have a pupil record ideas. Then pupils can work on their posters. You'll need to prepare some things ahead of time. Collect food coloring, white glue, cooking oil, cardboard or a piece of poster board for each pupil, 2 cups of cold cooked spaghetti. (To color the spaghetti, put in a few drops of food coloring and oil and toss together with a few drops of white glue.)

To make the posters, pupils can use the spaghetti to write (in cursive) the words *praise* or *glory* and then design a border. The pupils will form the words on the poster board, using the spaghetti, and then let it dry.

During *Sharing in Worship,* pupils can show their posters and finish the statement, "I can give glory to Jesus by . . . "

6. Psalm Prayer. Pupils will need Bibles, concordances, pencils, and copies of activity page 2B. This group will compose psalm prayers for the prayer during *Sharing in Worship.*

To begin, pupils should use concordances to look up Scripture references that include the word *praise.* Tell pupils to take their time and find verses they especially like. (You may want to have a few verses chosen just in case pupils can't decide.)

When we pray to God, we don't always have to ask Him for things. We can take the time to praise God for being who He is and for the wonderful things He does for us. Find a verse in Psalms that helps you praise God and

copy it on the page. Then use it to help you write your own prayer thoughts to God.

Sharing in Worship
● ● ● ● ● ● ● ● ● ● ● ● ● ● ● ●
(20-25 minutes)

Rearrange the suggested order of worship to include activities your pupils have prepared. Omit those not prepared by pupils.

Call to Worship (Group 1): **Group 1 has researched information on the word** *glory* **and how we can give glory to God today in our worship. Let's listen to that now.**

Music (Group 5): **Group 5 has compiled some songs that praise God.** Ask Group 5 to lead the group in singing or in choral reading.

Scripture (Group 2): Pupils can volunteer to read their diary entries about the Transfiguration. After they're finished, discuss their ideas.

Lord's Supper: God let His Son die on the cross for our sins. But He used His great power to bring Jesus back to life. We praise our God who has the power to heal and to create the Transfiguration.

Offering: God wants us to work with Him to help others. Let's worship God now by giving our money to help His church. Ask selected pupils to collect the offering.

Special Music (Group 3): **God has done many incredible things in peoples' lives. And God has the power to work wonderful events in our lives each day. Group 3 has an acrostic and a special song they want to sing that tells about this.** Group 3 shows their acrostic and sings the adaptation of "Bless the Lord, O My Soul."

Devotion (Group 4): **When we worship God, we praise Him. Group 4**

has prepared some praise posters and ideas on how they can praise God and Jesus. Group 4 shows their prayer posters and shares their ideas.

There are many ways to praise or give glory to God. When we sing or say our praise, we glorify God. Group 4 will lead or sing their songs at this time.

Today, we've discovered that the word *glorify* **means to praise, to show respect for, to honor, to love, to say good things about someone. God glorified Jesus at the Transfiguration. The disciples were awed and frightened by what they saw. We glorify Jesus by the things we say and do. When others see our lives, they will honor and glorify God, and we will be blessed by God!**

Prayer (Group 6): **Let's listen as group 6 reads their psalm prayers to conclude our worship time.** Group 6 will read their psalm prayers to the rest of the class. Ask for volunteers to read the prayers of praise to the Lord.

Closing Moments
● ● ● ● ● ● ● ● ● ● ● ● ● ● ● ●
(10-15 minutes)

Provide copies of activity page 3C, crayons or markers, pencils. Encourage pupils to put this page in the place where they usually have their quiet time. Pupils can finish the acrostic and review the memory verses. Beforehand record the memory verses on tape with some of the words missing. The pupils can say the words as they listen to the tape and work on their activity page.

Dear Diary

Try to put yourself in place of the apostles present at the Transfiguration.
How do you think you might have felt or reacted to all that happened?
Write a diary entry as you think one of the apostles might have written.

Dear Diary,
I can't believe what has happened . . . but I saw it with my own eyes.

_____

_____

_____

_____

_____

_____

_____

What will happen to me next as I work and learn from Jesus?
Signed,

Use a concordance to find
Scriptures that use the word "praise."
If you don't know how to use a concordance,
ask your teacher to help you. Once you have
found some praise verses, write psalm of praise
to God. If you need help getting started, look at
these Scriptures:

Psalm 8:1,2

Psalm 30:1-4

Psalm 33:1-3

Psalm 34:1-3

Psalm 42:5

Psalm 47:5-7

Dear God,

Because You _____ ,

_____ , and

_____ for me, I praise You.

To show You my love I will _____ ,

_____ , and

_____ .

Love,

raise

Building Blocks of Praise

Use this page to help you think of ways to praise God and to make praising Him a habit.

P
R
A
I
S
E

Prayer—
When you talk to God don't just ask Him for things or rattle off a list of "Blessmomanddadandgrandmas."

I can praise God in my prayers when I _____

_____

Reverence—
God derseves our praise because He is holy.

I can show God He is special to me by _____

_____

Adoration—
We should love God more than anyone else.

I can show God I adore Him when I _____

_____

Imitation—
Imitate Christ in what He said to God and in what He did.

I want to do as Jesus did by _____

_____

Singing—
Think of songs that express to God what He means to you.

List some here, then sing them to God. _____

_____

Exaltation—
God is more important than anything or anyone.

To show God how important He is to me, I will _____

_____

_____

3C

People Praise Jesus, God's Son

Worship Focus

Worship God because we love Him and His Son.

Transition Time

(10-15 minutes)

Send pupils to the rest room and water fountain. Then involve all pupils in the following activity.

Beforehand set up a "Memory" game in the classroom. Prepare twenty paper rock shapes. On each two paper rock shapes write a word of praise or a way to praise Jesus (sing, pray, shout, hallelujah, etc.).

Have all rocks turned face down so the words don't show. Number rocks from 1 to 20. Pupils can take turns choosing two numbers, turning over the rocks and checking to see if the words match. If the two rocks match, the pupil keeps that pair of rocks. (Or, to make it difficult, keep the rocks in the game.)

Launching the Theme

(10 minutes)

How can you tell someone how you feel about him or her? Let's think of some ways to do that, and list them here. (The teacher or a pupil recorder should write the ideas on the chalkboard or on a piece of poster board.) The list should include the following:

1. Write the person a note.
2. Give the person a present.
3. Tell the person you love her.
4. Do something nice for the person.
5. Make something for the person.

Since God is not here in bodily form with us right now, we can't do these things to show Him our love. We're going to talk about ways that we can tell God we love Him. We will do that today in several ways during our worship time. We will express our love and praise for God.

Building the Theme

(30 minutes)

1. Call to Worship. Pupils will read Psalm 47, paraphrase it, and then create an antiphonal reading for the Call to Worship.

Provide Bibles, paper, pencils, activity page 4A, Bible dictionary, and/or several versions of the Bible.

Have pupils turn to Psalm 47. Take time to read each verse and discuss it as a group. Use the Bible dictionary if there are words not known by the pupils. You may want to use several Bible translations to understand the phrases. Demonstrate how to go verse by verse and write an adaptation of the verses. For instance: "Clap your hands, all you nations; shout to God with cries of joy" could be adapted as "Clap and sing your own praise to God."

Depending on the size of the group, you could have each pupil rewrite an individual verse or have the group work together on all the verses. When the group has finished writing, decide how the group will present the psalm during *Sharing in Worship*. (Have all pupils read all verses, or have each pupil read one verse as a solo.)

One way we can show our love for God is to talk to Him. We will write our call to worship and then begin the service by telling God how important He is to us.

2. Scripture Play. Pupils will prepare the skit to show the Triumphal Entry. If possible, obtain real palm branches or have the pupils make them from green construction paper. To enhance the drama, have simple costumes such as robes, towels, and sashes. You may want to ask a teenager or adult to play the part of Jesus.

Give out copies of activity page 4B and pencils. Take a few moments to have people try out for parts, and then assign the parts.

This group needs to be off in an area where they can practice going through the skit. If necessary, rearrange the furniture or the room.

The skit will be presented during the Scripture portion of *Sharing in Worship*.

3. Special Music. This group will prepare a special song, "Clap Your Hands, All Ye Peoples," and will lead the group in singing other praise songs.

Provide paper, pencils, crayons or markers, hymnals or songbooks. It would be helpful to have blank overhead transparencies and transparency pens to write and display the words for the large group.

First, make sure all pupils know the song. If necessary, go over the words and melody, and write the words on an overhead transparency. This will be the special music during *Sharing in Worship*.

Then ask pupils to turn to the hymn, "Praise Him, Praise Him!" Go over the words and the tune to this song if necessary. Have pupils use paper and crayons or markers to illustrate some of the words in the first stanza (Jesus, earth, love, angel, shepherd, children, arms, etc.) Then, during the music portion of *Sharing in Worship*, the pupils can lead in "Clap Your Hands, All Ye Peoples," teach the chorus to the rest of the class, and show their illustrations when the group sings "Praise Him, Praise Him!"

Option: If you or your children do not know the song, "Clap Your Hands, All Ye Peoples," sing "Praise Him, Praise Him!" and any other praise songs you do know.

4. Offering Pennants. This group will prepare pennants to display during the offering portion of *Sharing in Worship*. Provide construction paper cut into the shape of triangles, plastic straws, crayons or markers, Bibles (several versions) and concordances.

Pupils should use the Bibles and concordances to look up words to describe and praise God. Use some of these words if you need to, to get pupils started: wonderful, great, fantastic, awesome, loving. Try to get a list of ten to fifteen words.

When you are looking for words to describe and praise the Lord, the Bible is the place to begin. Use the concordance (it's listed in ABC order) to help you look for words to describe God or Jesus. The concordance will also list particular verses with those words in them. Look up some of these verses and you will discover other descriptions of God and how we can praise Him.

Each pupil should choose one or two words and write them in large letters on the pennant. Ask pupils to decorate their pennants, and then demonstrate to pupils how to attach the paper to the straws for a handle.

During the offering time of *Sharing in Worship*, pupils will display their pennants, read their words, and tell why they think God is like that. Make sure you explain this to each pupil so he or she will know what to say during offering time.

5. Devotion. Pupils will decorate gift boxes to represent themselves and will be able to tell some special gifts or talents they have that they can use for God's work.

Provide small boxes (preferably with lids), wrapping paper, markers or crayons, old magazines, scissors, tape, paper and pencils.

All of us are special, because we all have different gifts and abilities that were given to us by God. Let's take a few moments to list three to five things you do well, or characteristics that describe you. You may need to provide some ideas to get the pupils started. (For instance, "I'm helpful.")

After several minutes, ask pupils to think about how they could use all of these abilities for God. You'll need to adapt as necessary. For instance, if someone says, "I like to talk," she might use that for God by talking to others about Him, or inviting someone to church. If someone says, "I like to babysit," he might want to babysit at church or babysit for someone else so that person could work at church.

Then have the pupils look for pictures, words, and so forth, from magazines, drawings, and calendars to put in the gift boxes to describe themselves (as if these gift boxes were themselves, as gifts to God).

Pupils should decorate the inside of their boxes with all of the information about themselves. Then they should wrap the outside of the boxes with wrapping paper. Make sure they have lids on the boxes or can still get inside the boxes to show off what they did.

These pupils will present their gift boxes of themselves during the devotional part of *Sharing in Worship*.

6. Prayer Partners. If possible, ask one of the church worship leaders to come in and talk to this group about why prayer is so important in worship. Then the small group of pupils will present this information during the prayer portion of *Sharing in Worship*.

If that's not possible, work with this group of pupils and train them so they can go back and lead other small groups of pupils in prayer. (This would be a good task for your 5th and 6th graders.)

Have this group make a list of three or four prayer concerns. Some possibilities might include praying for the ministers and church, praying for the pupils in the schools, praying for teachers and parents.

Prayer is an important part of our worship. When we pray we get the opportunity to tell God how great He is, thank Him for all He's done for us, and ask Him for favors. You will be leading a small group of pupils in prayer today.

Make sure these pupils understand that they are to lead the small group in prayer. Let them know that the other members in the group will have a responsibility too.

Sharing in Worship

Call to Worship (Group 1): Group 1 has prepared an antiphonal call to worship. Let's listen as they read now. Group 1 does their reading of Psalm 47.

Music (Group 3): Group 3 has prepared a special number for us. Have Group 3 sing "Clap Your Hands, All Ye Peoples" and teach the chorus to the other pupils. Then Group 3 should lead the group in singing the hymn, "Praise Him, Praise Him." Make sure the pupils in this group show the illustrations for the words in the song.

Scripture (Group 2): The members of Group 2 have practiced a skit of the Triumphal Entry. Let's listen as they present it now. After the group has presented the skit, lead the group in a discussion of the different attitudes of people present at this event.

Lord's Supper: Let's take this time now to think about all the ways God shows us He loves us. The greatest way He showed His love was when He sent Jesus to die for us. Talk to God right now and ask for forgiveness if there are things you need help with.

Offering (Group 4): Group 4 has prepared some pennants with words to worship God. While the offering is being passed by a couple of pupils, this group can show their pennants and tell why they think God can be described by their words on the pennants.

Devotion (Group 5): At the beginning of the session, we talked about ways we could show someone we loved him. One way we listed was to give a present to someone. Group 5 has prepared a unique way to show how we can present ourselves as gifts to God.

Group 5 open their gift boxes and show themselves as gifts for God. Make sure they tell how they can use their abilities or personality traits for God.

Most of you probably don't think of yourselves as gift-wrapped packages to God! But, in a way, that's really what you are. God has made each of us unique and special. Although we are all very different from each other, each of us has talents and abilities that can be used for God. And that is how God works in this world—through us! With the talents we have, we can reach out to other people—our friends and families—and show God's love to them.

Every ability or talent is important. You can talk, write, sing, read, help, all kinds of things. And each time you come to church you are learning more.

And that is a very important reason to praise God and show Him that we love Him. When we say "yes" to God and to what He wants us to do, we are giving Him the best gift of all—ourselves.

Prayer (Group 6): The members of Group 6 will be leading in small group prayers at this time. (Divide the group as quickly and quietly as possible. Then allow time for Group 6 members to lead in prayer. Close the prayer time yourself.)

Closing Moments

Provide copies of activity page 4C and pencils. Encourage the pupils to think of gifts and abilities they have, and write about them in the space in the gift box.

If there's extra time, ask the groups to design cheers for God. If anyone in the group is a cheerleader, he or she could help give some guidelines. Review the Bible story about how the people shouted praises to God. Then see if the group can come up with a cheer to shout their own praises to God.

Psalm 47 — Shouts of Praise!

Read Psalm 47 and decide how you can write your own praise to God.
On the blank lines paraphrase the verses that are given.
Then assign parts to read your psalm as a group.

Verse 1—
Clap your hands, all you nations; shout to God with cries of joy.

READER 1: _____

_____

_____

ALL: Shout to God with songs of praise!

Verse 2—
How awesome is the Lord Most High, the great King over all the earth!

READER 2: _____

_____

_____

ALL: Shout to God with songs of praise!

Verse 6—
Sing praises to God, sing praises; sing praises to our King, sing praises.

DUET: _____

_____

_____

ALL: Shout to God with songs of praise!

Verse 7—
For God is the King of all the earth; sing to him a psalm of praise.

TRIO: _____

_____

_____

ALL: Shout to God with songs of praise!

Verse 8—
God reigns over the nations; God is seated on his holy throne.

READER 1: _____

_____

_____

ALL: Shout to God with songs of praise!

• •

• •

• •

• •

Radio Report

Read this skit in your group.
Assign parts and practice before performing it.

Characters: reporter, Pharisee, John the disciple, woman in the crowd

Reporter: This is Sarah (Joseph) bar Zebedee, from station WJRS. Excitement is high in Jerusalem today as people crowd the streets to welcome the teacher-rabbi Jesus of Nazareth. Let's see if we can talk to some people in the crowd...Sir, sir, may we speak to you for a moment?

Pharisee: What do you want? Can't you see I'm busy?

Reporter: Would you tell our listening audience what you think of this Jesus of Nazareth?

Pharisee: A troublemaker, that's what He is! I tried to force Him to make these people be quiet, but He said He could make the stones speak! He dares to compare himself with God! A blasphemer! A fool!

Reporter: Uh, thank you for your comment, sir. There's John, a disciple and close friend of Jesus. John, could we speak to you for a minute?

John: Sure, but for just a minute. Isn't this exciting? All of these people are here to praise the Master! It's been an incredible day! And Jesus knew about all this ahead of time. He even sent two of us ahead to get a donkey for Him to ride on. This is, indeed, a wonderful day! Don't you agree?

Reporter: I can't comment; I'm supposed to be objective, you know. Thanks for your time, John. Let's make our way into the crowd to see who else is here. Ma'am, what do you think of this Jesus?

Woman: He's really here! The Messiah has come, just as the prophets said. Blessed is He who comes in the name of the Lord. Hosanna!

Reporter: There you have it—three eyewitnesses commenting on the teacher-rabbi Jesus. (Beginning to shout into microphone) The noise level is incredible here! I'm having trouble getting through the immense crowd. This is Sarah (Joseph) bar Zebedee—from station WJRS—signing—off!

My Gift to God

What gifts, talents, and abilities do you have that make you special? Write some in the blanks on this gift box. Think about ways you can use your special abilities for God.

I like to_____

_____

_____

_____

_____

I am good at_____

_____

_____

_____

_____

I feel I am _____

_____

_____

_____

People tell me I have a talent for _____

_____

_____

_____

I can use my gifts, talents, and abilities for God by_____

_____

_____

_____

_____

_____

_____

_____

_____

Jesus Dies

Worship Focus

Worship God because He sent His Son, Jesus, to die for us.

Transition Time

(10 minutes)

Send the children in small groups to the rest room and drinking fountain. Welcome newcomers and involve everyone in the following activity.

Graffiti: For this activity, tape a large piece of newsprint paper to a flat wall. Provide markers or crayons. As the children arrive, have them decorate the paper with graffiti. At the top of the paper, have the title, "Things God Has Done for Us." The children may write words or draw pictures of these times.

Launching the Theme

(10 minutes)

Have the children sit where they can see the "graffiti" wall they just created. **What are some of the things you wrote that God has done for you?** Allow pupils to share about things God has given them or done for them. If anyone wrote "Jesus," focus on this. If not, name Jesus as the most special gift God has given us. **God's Son, Jesus, was the best gift God could ever have given us. Does anyone know why Jesus was such a special gift?** (Allow response.) **Jesus did something just for you and me that was very difficult to do. He died for us. Today we're going to worship God because He sent Jesus to die for us.**

Briefly explain the choices of preparation for worship. You may allow the pupils to choose the group in which they would like to participate.

Building the Theme

(30 minutes)

1. Call to Worship. Before the session, have the words to the song, "Jesus, the Son of God," printed on poster board. (See page 40.)

Have the children sing through the song a few times to become comfortable with teaching it to the whole group during *Sharing in Worship.* For a challenge activity, have the pupils write another verse to the song to teach to the group.

Focus a discussion on what the words mean. **What does this song tell us that God did?** (He sent His Son.) **Why did He do this?** (To show us His great love.) **(What did Jesus do?** (Died.) **Why did Jesus die for us?** (To give us life.) **What are we to do as a result of Jesus' death?** (Follow Jesus.)

2. Scripture. For this activity you will need Bibles, pencils, and activity page 5A. Have the pupils read Mark 14:43-50, 63-65; 15:26-28, 33-39. On the activity page are two columns. In one column pupils will list as many things as they can find that show man's apparent power over God in the death of Jesus. In the other column have them list things that show how God's greater power is demonstrated in Jesus' death. You may suggest prophecies that were fulfilled as evidence of God's power (Psalm 22:18; 22:7, 8; Isaiah 53:12; Psalm 22:1; Psalm 69:21).

Focus a discussion on helping the children understand that, although it seemed as if man overpowered God at one point, it is obvious God has the ultimate power. **Let's look up Mark 14:43-50, 63-65; 15:26-28, 33-39 and read these verses to ourselves.** (Do so.) **What events seem to show that man had power over God in the death of Jesus?** (Allow response.) **It seemed as if man had more power when Judas betrayed Jesus and the soldiers arrested Jesus. Men told lies about Jesus so He would be found guilty of blasphemy. He was beaten and finally nailed to a cross. He had a long and painful death. These happenings make it appear that man had more power than God because man killed God's Son, Jesus.**

But then some other events occurred that showed us that God always was in control. What were some of these events? (Allow response.) **God caused darkness to fall during daylight hours. The temple curtain was torn as Jesus**

died. This event also fulfilled prophecies made many years earlier. Look up the Scriptures given on your activity page. These verses all tell of prophecies to fulfill in later years. And they were fulfilled when Jesus died. Jesus' death was all part of God's plan made long ago. Man never had more power than God. Jesus allowed himself to be killed as part of God's plan.

3. Devotion. For this activity you will need a roll of shelf paper and art supplies for the children to draw a mural illustrating the events of Jesus' death. Have the children read Mark 15:21-28, 33-39. As they read, have them write down the events in the order they occurred. Then they may use the art supplies to illustrate the events. During the devotional talk, they can display the mural.

4. Scripture. This activity could be a self-explanatory/challenge activity. No teacher help is needed if you wish. For this activity you will need activity page 5B, Bibles, and pencils.

Have the children look up and read the verses found on their activity page. The first group of verses tells how we are all sinners. The second group of verses tells how our sins are forgiven. The third group tells us what our response to this should be. The pupils are to re-write these verses in a way that makes it more personal to them. (For example: Romans 3:23 says, "All have sinned." It could be re-written as, "I have [or Jane has] sinned," and so on.)

If you wish to include teacher help, focus a discussion on helping the children understand why it was such a great gift for God to send Jesus to die for us. **What do the verses in the first group tell us?** (We are all sinners and the price for sin is death.) **What did God do to help us in this situation?** (Sent Jesus to die for us.) **Jesus' death paid for what?** (Our sins.)

Because of Jesus, what happened to our sins? (They are all forgiven.) **Since our sins are forgiven, what does this mean?** (We are made holy and righteous. We can be in the presence of God.) **In the last group of verses, what does God's Word tell us we should do about Jesus' death paying for our sins?** (Tell others so they will know; forgive others since God forgave us.) **Write these verses, putting your name or "I" or "me" in to make the verses more personal to you.**

5. **Personal Praise.** For this activity have the children write endings to the open-ended stories found on activity page 5C. During *Sharing in Worship* they can act out the stories as skits. The purpose of this activity is for the children to think of ways forgiveness can be shown.

Before writing, focus a discussion on helping the pupils understand forgiveness. **Think of a time when you sinned. Maybe you said something bad about someone or didn't do your best job on something your parents asked you to do. Think how bad you felt. Now think of how you felt when someone said, "That's okay. Forget it." Isn't it a wonderful feeling to be forgiven? We also can forgive. If others do something to hurt us or make us feel bad, we can forgive them, just as we have been forgiven. God has forgiven our sins when we didn't deserve to be forgiven. We should forgive others the same way.**

6. **Prayer.** For this activity provide paper and pencils. Have the children write a short paragraph telling what Jesus' death means to them. At the end of *Sharing in Worship* some of the pupils could read their paragraphs aloud. After those have shared who wished to, have the pupils form a prayer circle. Have pupils pray aloud if they wish. Have them emphasize thanks to God for sending His Son, Jesus, to die for them.

Sharing in Worship

● ● ● ● ● ● ● ● ● ● ● ● ● ● ● ●

(30 minutes)

Omit any of the following sections if you did not offer the corresponding activity.

Call to Worship (Group 1): Have the group sing the song, "Jesus, the Son of God." Have them teach it to the group along with the new verse they wrote.

Devotion (Group 3): **Group 3 illustrated the events of Jesus' death. As we have our devotional talk, they will display their mural.**

Devotional Talk: We are worshiping God today because He sent His Son, Jesus, to die for us. Jesus never sinned while He was on earth, yet the chief priests and the teachers of the law tried to find evidence against Jesus so He could be killed. Men told lies about Jesus so He would be found guilty. He was beaten, mocked, and people shouted insults at Him. They nailed Him to a cross and hung Him to die between two robbers. He was offered vinegar to drink and they cast lots to see who would get His clothes.

Then God sent darkness during the daylight time. Jesus cried out, "My God, my God, why have You forsaken me?" When Jesus finally died, the curtain in the temple was torn in two from top to bottom. A centurion who had seen how Jesus died said, "Surely this man was the Son of God."

Was God defeated? Did He have a plan that man overpowered by killing Jesus? (Allow response.) **No! God had planned from the very beginning to send His Son to die for us. God knew that you and I would be sinners. God and sin cannot be together. God is holy and fair, and sin must be paid for. Someone had to pay for our sins. God loved us so much that He sent His Son, Jesus, to pay for our sins. Jesus painfully died on that**

cross in our place. Because of this, we are forgiven of our sins. We are now able to be with God. Jesus could have decided He didn't want to suffer and die, but He loved us enough to do it. Thank God He sent Jesus to die for us so our sins could be forgiven and we can be with Him forever!

Scripture (Group 2): We heard in our devotion time how Jesus was killed. It seemed as if God was not as powerful as man when Jesus suffered and died. Group 2 is going to share with us times when it seemed man was more powerful and then times when it was obvious God was and always had been in control. Have the children share their findings.

Lord's Supper: Jesus' death was part of God's plan for us. God loved us so much He wanted us to be able to come into His presence. As sinners, this was impossible. Our sins had to be paid for—blood needed to be shed. Jesus allowed himself to be beaten and killed, so we could be forgiven. Let's think of these events as we partake in the Lord's Supper.

Offering: God gave us the best that He had by sending Jesus to die for us. We should give Him back our best, whether it be our time or our money. As we give our offerings to God, let's think about ways we can give Him our best.

Scripture (Group 4): Group 4 did research on why it was such a great gift for God to send Jesus to die for us. They will share verses about ourselves, what happened when Jesus died, and what we should do as a response to Him.

Personal Praise (Group 5): Group 5 has written endings to some short stories showing forgiveness. They are going to act out these stories as short skits. Have pupils act out skits. If time permits, you could have group discussion on other possible endings.

Prayer (Group 6): Group 6 has written paragraphs telling what Jesus' death means to them. After they share their writings we will close with a group circle prayer. Let's thank God for sending Jesus to die for us. Because of Jesus' death, we are now able to spend eternity with God.

Closing Moments
● ● ● ● ● ● ● ● ● ● ● ● ● ● ●
(10 minutes)

Write the following words on a chalkboard or poster board, scrambling the letters. Tell the children the words are from today's worship time. See how many words can be unscrambled in a limited amount of time. (Words are: cross, blasphemy, curtain, darkness, prophecies, centurion, forgiven.) If time permits, add more words to the list. If you have younger children in your group, you may want to use some easier words than these.

D.W.   Don Whitman

1. Je - sus, the Son of God   Came from Heav'n a - bove;
2. Je - sus, the Son of God,   Lord of life was He;
3. Je - sus, the Son of God   Died up - on the cross.
4. Je - sus, the Son of God,   We will fol - low Thee.

Sent to us from God on high To show us His great love.
Healed the blind and raised the dead, That we His pow'r might see.
Lives a - gain to give us life If we will in Him trust.
Tell us what to do and say And help us true to be.

© 1958 by Don Whitman. Used by permission.

Evidence of God's Power

When Jesus died on the cross, it appeared as though He were a loser—that man had triumphed over Him. But was He a loser? No way! Read the Scriptures listed on this page. On the left side of the cross, note the events that make it seem as though man had power. On the right side of the cross, list evidence that God was (and is) in control, and that He has the greatest power.

God's Power:

Psalm 22:1

Psalm 22:18

Isaiah 53:12

Mark 14:43-50

Mark 14:63-65

Mark 15:26-28
Psalm 22:7, 8

Mark 15:33-39
Psalm 69:21

Man's Power:

Mark 14:43-50

Mark 14:63-65

Mark 15:26-28

Mark 15:33-39

Consider Yourself

Look up the following verses about sin and forgiveness. Read the verse, then rewrite it or paraphrase it to make the message more personal to you. *(Hint: Use your name, or the words "I" or "me.")* One verse in each group has been done for you as an example.

Sin

Romans 3:23   **Romans 5:12**   **1 John 1:10**

Romans 5:8   **Romans 6:23**

But God demonstrates his own love for me, Shanda Maxwell, in this: while I was still a sinner, Christ died for me.

Forgiveness

1 John 1:9   **2 Corinthians 5:21**

God made him who had no sin, Jesus, to be sin for me, Andre Wilson, so that in him I might become the righteousness of God.

Hebrews 10:10   **1 John 1:7**

What I Can Do

Matthew 28:19, 20   **Matthew 6:14, 15**

Luke 6:37   **Colossians 3:13**

I, Chris Tucker, should bear with others and forgive whatever grievances I have against someone else. I should forgive as the Lord Jesus Christ forgave me.

God sent Jesus to die for our sins, even though we didn't deserve to be forgiven. We should learn to forgive others. How can the different characters in the stories below show forgiveness? Write an ending to each story, describing how forgiveness could be shown. Then prepare to act out the stories for your group.

1

Carl and David mowed grass during the summer to earn some extra money. One day they were trying to hurry so they could go to the state fair. When they mowed Mrs. Carter's yard, they did a very sloppy job. Since she was elderly and unable to see where they missed mowing in places, Mrs. Carter paid the boys their usual amount.

Carl and David felt _____

_____

Mrs. Carter _____

_____

2

Melissa, Robin, and Allison were best friends. They liked to do things together. But Melissa was jealous whenever Robin and Allison did things together without including her. Melissa told Robin a lie about Allison, hoping Robin would no longer want to be Allison's friend. Allison found out about the lie.

Allison told _____

_____

Then Melissa _____

_____

3

Derek's dad found one of his tools out in the yard where it shouldn't have been. It had been rained on and had begun to rust. Derek's dad was angry and thought Derek had left the tool in the yard. Derek tried to explain that he didn't leave it out, but his dad punished him anyway.

Derek was _____

_____

His dad _____

_____

Finish the Story

5C

Jesus Lives!

Worship Focus

Worship God because He brought His Son, Jesus, back to life.

Transition Time

(10 minutes)

Send the children in small groups to the rest room and drinking fountain. Welcome newcomers and involve everyone in the following activity.

Verse Scramble: Have the following words written on index cards: But God / raised Him / from the dead, / freeing him / from the agony / of death, / because it / was impossible / for death / to keep / its hold / on him. / Acts 2:24. Write each word group twice on separate cards. Divide the children into two teams. Give each group a set of the index cards. Each person should have one card. When you signal, have each team arrange itself in the correct order of the verse. If you don't have enough children to do this, each team may lay out the cards on the floor in the correct order.

Launching the Theme

(10 minutes)

How many of you have attended a funeral? How did you feel? (Allow children to share.) **People are usually sad at funerals. Even if we know the person was a Christian and will be with God, we are sad because we will miss that person.**

Last week we talked about the death of Jesus. Many people loved Him and were sad about His suffering and eventual death. Jesus didn't deserve to die, yet He was tortured and hung on a cross. How do you feel about Jesus' death? (Allow response.) **God's plan was to bring Jesus back to life three days after His death. How do you think you would have felt if you had gone to Jesus' tomb and found it empty?** (Allow response.) **God did raise Jesus from the dead, and this has a very special meaning to you and to me! Today we are worshiping God because He brought his Son, Jesus, back to life.**

Briefly explain the choices of preparation for worship. You may allow the pupils to choose which group in which they would like to participate.

Building the Theme
●●●●●●●●●●●●●●●●
(30 minutes)

1. Call to Worship. For this activity use activity page 6A and provide pencils. On the activity page is the acrostic, "JESUS LIVES!" Have the pupils write a line for each letter about Jesus' death and resurrection. For example:

Jesus died for me
I lovE Him
HiS death was a sad time.
BUt He came back to life!
BecauSe of Him, I can go to Heaven.

Jesus is aLive today.
I will praise and thank Him.
He died for eVeryone's sins.
I beliEve in Jesus.
He is God's Son.

During *Sharing in Worship,* the group can present the acrostic as a responsive reading. The group can say the line in the acrostic, then all the children will respond with "Jesus lives!"

As the children are writing the acrostic, help them to think of lines to write by discussing Jesus' death and resurrection. **Why did Jesus die?** (Allow response.) **He was unfairly put to death because He claimed to be God's Son. Why did He allow this to happen? It was God's plan so our sins can be forgiven. Why do you think it is important that Jesus was brought back to life?** (Allow response.) **It means what He said is true. He really is God's Son. He was victorious over death, so I can be victorious over death too.**

2. Devotion. For this activity the children will act out a skit telling the events of the resurrection. Have them read John 20:1-18 to know the events. You may wish to include a few props such as strips of cloth and a folded cloth. If your time is limited or your group is very small, omit this activity and use the devotional thoughts only.

3. Scripture. For this activity you will need copies of activity page 6B, pencils, and Bibles.

Have the children look up the verses found on their activity pages. After they have completed their pages, focus a discussion on the meaning of the verses. **Why did Christ die?** (Because of my sins.) **What happened after He died?** (He was buried and raised from the dead on the third day.) **What does this mean will happen to me?** (I will be made alive in Christ.) **Who or which is more powerful, death or Christ? How do we know this?** (Allow response.) **Yes, Christ is more powerful. He was stronger than death when He came back to life. Death cannot be victorious any more. Jesus proved that. I can also be victorious over eternal death.**

4. Music. For this activity you will need the words to the song, "He Is Lord," written on a poster board; another piece of poster board, and a marker. Have the children look up Philippians 2:10, 11. Have the group practice singing "He Is Lord" a couple of times. Then have the children write new verses to the same tune. These verses should tell what Jesus' resurrection means to them. Write the new verses on the poster board. During *Sharing in Worship* the group can teach the song to the entire group.

Focus a discussion on helping the children understand the words. **Who is Lord?** (Jesus.) **What miracle does this song tell us about Jesus?** (He is risen from the dead.) **What does the verse tell us will eventually occur?** (All people will bow and confess that Jesus is Lord.) **What does it mean to be Lord?** (Allow response.) **It means to have supreme authority. If Jesus is, indeed, our Lord,** we will obey Him in all areas of our lives. Words to "He Is Lord":

He Is Lord; He Is Lord;
He is risen from the dead, and He is Lord.
Ev'ry knee shall bow, every tongue
  confess
That Jesus Christ is Lord.

If you do not know this song, use a hymn such as "Wounded for Me," or verse 3 of "Tell Me the Story of Jesus." Discuss the meaning of these words to help the children understand why Jesus died and why the resurrection is so important to us.

5. Personal Praise. For this activity you will need construction paper, scissors, glue, glitter, scraps of fabric, and markers. Have the children create cards to give to someone who doesn't know Jesus. The cards should show joy and excitement felt because of the resurrection of Jesus. **How do you think Mary and Peter must have felt when Jesus was killed?** (Allow response.) **How do you think they felt when they learned He was alive again? Can you imagine seeing Jesus face to face and having Him call you by name? What would you have said to Him?** (Allow response.) **We know Jesus' resurrection means He was victorious over death. This means we also can have that victory. We should be full of joy and excitement and thankfulness that Jesus is alive! One way we can show our thankfulness and joy is by sharing this news with people who don't know Jesus. Think of someone you can send your card to who needs to know about Jesus' death and resurrection.**

6. Prayer. For this activity you will need heavy construction paper or tagboard, markers, and pens. Have the children create bookmarks for the entire group. The bookmark should tell about Jesus' resurrection. An illustration could be drawn or a verse could be written and decorated. At the close of *Sharing in Worship,* during prayer time, the bookmarks can be shared and distributed to the children.

Focus a discussion on being thankful to God for bringing Jesus back to life. **Why is it important that Jesus came back to life?** (Allow response.) **Jesus overcame death. He is more powerful than death. Everything He said is true. He is the Son of God. Our sins are forgiven. We can also overcome death. We have absolutely nothing to fear.**

Sharing in Worship
● ● ● ● ● ● ● ● ● ● ● ● ● ● ● ●
(25-30 minutes)

Omit any of the following sections if you did not offer the corresponding activity.

Call to Worship (Group 1): Have the group present their acrostic, "Jesus Lives," as a responsive reading. **Group 1 wrote an acrostic for the words, "Jesus Lives." They will say a line of the acrostic and we will all say the words, "Jesus lives!" together. We can worship God with our responsive reading.**

Devotion (Group 2): **Group 2 is going to present a skit based on the Scripture, John 20:1-18. This Scripture tells us the story of Jesus' resurrection.** Have the group present the skit.

Devotional Talk: We just saw the events of the morning when Jesus was first seen alive after His death. Put yourself in Mary or Peter's place. What would you have thought if you had seen Jesus' tomb empty, with only the folded cloth and strips of linen in it? (Allow response.) **They probably thought His body had been stolen, according to what Mary said to the man she believed to be the gardener. When Mary realized she**

was talking to Jesus, how do you think she felt?

It truly was a miracle for God to bring Jesus back to life. Why is this important to you and me? (Allow response.) **God had a plan from the very beginning. He knew you and I would be sinners. As sinners, we were unable to be in God's presence since God and sin cannot dwell together. Someone had to pay for those sins. God sent Jesus to pay that price. Jesus died so our sins could be forgiven.**

But if Jesus had stayed dead in the tomb, God's plan would not have been completed. Jesus said He would be raised in three days, and He was! **Jesus had more power than even death. We know everything Jesus said is true. Our sins have been paid for. And since Jesus had victory over death, we have the assurance that we will be victorious over death! We have the assurance that we will spend eternity with God in Heaven. We have nothing to fear, not even death! Praise God for His wonderful plan of bringing Jesus back to life!**

Scripture (Group 3): **Group 3 read some verses in their Bibles and then rewrote the verses in their own words.** Have the children take turns reading the verses from their Bibles and then reading their paraphrases.

Lord's Supper: **Jesus allowed himself to suffer and die for us. The blood He shed washes away our sins. Because our sins are forgiven, we also can be victorious over death, just as Jesus was. Let's thank God for bringing Jesus back to life as we participate in the Lord's Supper.**

Offering: **God gave us His very best by sending Jesus to earth. One way we can show our thankfulness to God is by giving our offerings to Him.**

Music (Group 4): **Group 4 is going to lead us in singing the song, "He Is Lord." They have also written some new** verses to the song about Jesus' being alive again. Have the group sing this song, or another of your choice, including the new verses.

Personal Praise (Group 5): **Group 5 created some cards telling about the resurrection of Jesus. They will share these with us now.** Have each pupil share his card. **There are many ways to tell others about Jesus' being alive again. The people in this group are going to give their cards to someone who doesn't know Jesus. We all have the responsibility to tell others about Jesus. Making cards to give to people is one way we can do this.**

Prayer (Group 6): Have the entire group form a circle. **Group 6 created bookmarks for everyone to remind us that Jesus is alive. You can use these bookmarks in your Bibles. Every time you read your Bible you can take a moment to thank God for bringing Jesus back to life.** Have the bookmarks distributed. Then close with prayer. Have pupils who wish to pray aloud do so.

Closing Moments
● ● ● ● ● ● ● ● ● ● ● ● ● ● ● ● ●
(10 minutes)

For this activity you will need drawing paper and markers or crayons.

We are worshiping God today for bringing Jesus back to life. We are filled with joy and excitement because of this miracle. It means we have a LIVING Lord and Savior. On your paper, create a joy picture. We can worship God by creating pictures for Him. We can also use our pictures to share Jesus' resurrection with those who don't know Jesus. Your picture can be joyful colors or a specific picture or anything you want to create to show how you feel about Jesus' being alive!

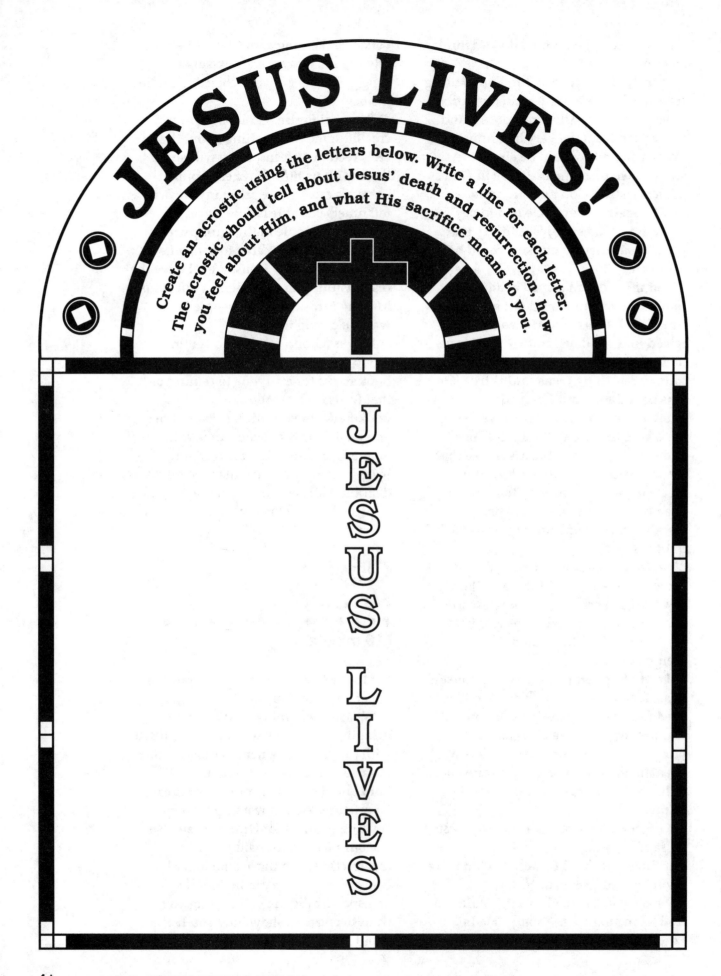

JESUS LIVES!

Create an acrostic using the letters below. Write a line for each letter. The acrostic should tell about Jesus' death and resurrection, how you feel about Him, and what His sacrifice means to you.

J
E
S
U
S

L
I
V
E
S

Christ's Victory — Our Victory

The verses below tell about Jesus' resurrection and how we can have eternal life because of His sacrifice. Look up the verses and fill in the blanks. Then find those words in the puzzle. The words can be horizontal, vertical, or diagonal, forwards or backwards.

1 Corinthians 15:3, 4

"Christ _____ for our _____ according to the _____ , that he was _____ , that he was _____ on the _____ day. . ."

1 Corinthians 15:21, 22

"For since _____ came through a _____ , the _____ of the dead comes also _____ a man. For as in _____ all die, so in _____ all will be made _____ ."

1 Corinthians 5:47, 49

"The _____ man was of the _____ of the _____ , the _____ man from _____ . And just as we have borne the _____ of the _____ man, so shall we _____ the likeness of the man from heaven."

1 Corinthians 15:51, 52

". . . We will not all _____ , but we will all be _____ — in a _____ , in the _____ of an _____ at the last _____ . For the trumpet will _____ , the dead will be raised _____ , and we will all be changed."

1 Corinthians 15:57

"But _____ be to _____ ! He gives us the _____ through our _____ _____ Christ."

"He is not here;
he has risen,
just as he said.
Come and see
the place where
he lay."

Matthew 28:6

```
I M P E R I S H A B L E N
T A P A D U S T M E Q A O
W D S R Z R E A B A T R I
I A O T S I N S D R R T T
N L U H S L E E P G U H C
K J N Q U M K S O D M L E
L F D T S R I F E Y P Y R
I L R Y E A L I V E E V R
N A I W J B D H K S T A U
G S H S E R U T P I R C S
Z H T A E D N O C E S X E
B U R I E D O D E S I A R
T H R O U G H E A V E N J
N V I C T O R Y S I P G N
S T R N H D E G N A H C G
C H R I S T H A N K S X Y
```

Jesus Appears

Worship Focus

Worship God because He provided opportunities for people to see Jesus alive again.

Transition Time
(10 minutes)

Send the children in small groups to the rest room and drinking fountain. Welcome newcomers and involve everyone in the following activity.

Guess the Object: For this activity you will need several blindfolds and two identical bags of objects. Form two teams. One team will try to identify objects by feel only. The other team will identify them by sight. Have the teams compete to see who identifies the objects first. Blindfold the children who will identify by feel only. Have the children who can see identify the objects by writing on the chalkboard what the objects are. Each blindfolded child should reach into the bag and pull out one object. He may feel the object but not see it. Do not return the objects to the bag for the next child's turn. Make this a relay game.

How many of you could immediately identify the object you chose? Why did the other team always finish first? Yes, because they could see what they were holding. Seeing something is far better than just feeling it, or hearing about it.

Launching the Theme
(10 minutes)

Have you ever had someone tell you something that was hard to believe? (Allow pupils to share "hard to believe" stories.) **When we can see something with our own eyes, it is easier to identify it or to believe in it.**

When man first walked on the moon, many people did not believe it, even though they saw it on TV. They thought the whole thing was staged. (Some people still don't believe this really happened!) Seeing this on TV wasn't the same as seeing it in person. When Jesus was raised from the dead, people saw with their own eyes.

When Jesus rose from the dead, do you think everyone who heard about it believed it? (Allow response.) God knew people would have trouble believing Jesus was alive if no one actually saw Him alive after His death. God provided times when human beings could actually see Jesus alive again after His death.

These people were witnesses—that is, they could tell others that they had seen Him alive. Today we are worshiping God for providing those opportunities for people to see that Jesus is alive.

Briefly explain the choices of preparation for worship. You may allow the pupils to choose the group in which they would like to participate.

Building the Theme
• • • • • • • • • • • • • • • • •
(30 minutes)

1. Call to Worship. For this activity you will need a large piece of fabric, fabric scraps, scissors, sequins, yarn, glitter, markers, and glue. The children will create a banner to display in the classroom during *Sharing in Worship*. The banner should express the children's joy and excitement because of their belief that Jesus is alive.

How do you feel when you see a friend you haven't seen in a long time? (Allow response.) **How do you think Jesus' friends felt when they saw Him alive again after they had seen Him die?** (Allow response.) **They were probably very happy to see Him again, because they loved Him. They were especially glad that He was alive again after they had seen Him die. We, too, can believe that Jesus is alive. We should be filled with joy and excitement because of this. Let's try to make our banner show how we know Jesus is alive and how we feel about it.**

2. Devotion. For this activity you will need a small box for each child, construction paper, scissors, glue, markers, and Bibles. Have the children read John 21:1-14 in their Bibles. Then have each pupil create a diorama showing part of the story that was just read. During the devotional talk the children can display their dioramas in sequence to give their account of the story from the Scriptures.

3. Scripture. For this activity you will need activity page 7A for each pupil, scissors, pencils, markers, and Bibles. Have each child cut apart the pages on the dotted lines on his activity page. Each page has a Scripture passage written on it. The child should read the verses, decide who Jesus appeared to, write it on the page, and illustrate it. When the pages are done, staple them together to form a book.

Before beginning, focus a short discussion on Jesus' appearances after His resurrection. **Why do you think Jesus appeared to some people, such as His disciples, after He rose from the dead?** (Allow response.) **I'm sure it helped people to believe He really was alive again. It helps us, also, to believe that Jesus is alive. Witnesses saw Him alive again with their own eyes, and then told others or wrote about it. There are many places in our Bibles where people have written about seeing Jesus alive. We can share these testimonies with others to help them believe too.**

4. Music. For this activity you will need the words and music to the chorus of the song, "He Lives," poster board, and marker. Have these words to the chorus printed on the poster board so the children can read them.

> He lives, He lives, Christ Jesus lives today!
> He walks with me and talks with me along life's narrow way.
> He lives, He lives, salvation to bestow.
> You ask me how I know He lives? The Bible tells me so!

Have the pupils learn the song to sing during *Sharing in Worship*. Have them write another chorus to the song. The words should be about Jesus' being alive again. Write the new words on the same poster board.

How do we know Jesus lives? (Allow response.) **We know Jesus is alive because our Bibles tell us this is true. Our Bibles tells us about people who actually saw Jesus alive. He appeared to many people after His resurrection. We can be assured Jesus is alive today!**

5. Personal Praise. For this activity you will need activity page 7B. On this page are open-ended situations. The children are to read a situation and decide how they would respond. These may be acted out as skits during *Sharing in Worship.*

How do *you* know Jesus is alive today? (Allow response.) **Our Bibles tell us, people have actually seen Him and written about it in our Bibles, and we have experienced Jesus' help and love. Do you think it is important for us to tell other people that Jesus is alive? Why?** (Allow response.) **They need to know Jesus died for their sins too, so they can be forgiven and spend eternity with Him. They need to know it didn't all end when Jesus was killed. They need to know our Lord is alive today and is able to help us.**

6. Scripture. For this activity you will need activity page 7C and pencils. Have the pupils look up the verses on their page and write down ways Jesus helps us. These should reinforce the fact that Jesus is alive since He has provided these blessings.

We know Jesus is alive because our Bibles tell us so. Our Bibles contain verses that tell about times when Jesus appeared alive to people after His death. We also know Jesus is alive because He helps us and provides things we need. On your activity page are verses that tell us things Jesus provides for us. If Jesus were not alive, we wouldn't have the

assurance of these blessings. Jesus is alive and is always with us. He knows our every need and takes care of us.

Sharing in Worship
• • • • • • • • • • • • • • • •
(30 minutes)

Omit any of the following sections if you did not offer the corresponding activity.

Call to Worship (Group 1): **Group 1 has created a banner to display showing the joy and excitement they have because of their belief that Jesus is alive.** Have the children hold up the banner while they tell about it. After they have finished, place the banner somewhere in the classroom for the remainder of this unit.

Devotion (Group 2): Have the members of Group 2 share their dioramas during the devotional talk. The children should be able to look at them as you share with them about today's Scriptures.

Devotional Talk: Simon Peter and some of the other disciples had been out fishing all night. They caught no fish. They were probably tired and discouraged. Early in the morning they saw a man standing on the shore. The man called out and said, "Friends, haven't you any fish?" They answered, "No." The man told them to throw their net on the right side of the boat and they would find some. How do you think the disciples may have felt when this man told them they would catch fish when they had tried all night and had caught nothing? (Allow response.)

When the disciples heard this command, they may have remembered back to another time when they had fished all night and caught no fish (Luke 5:1-11). Jesus had climbed into Simon Peter's boat and told him to put the boat out into deep water and to let

down the nets for a catch. When they did, they caught so many fish that their nets began to break. It was at that time that the disciples were told to leave everything and follow Jesus because now they were going to catch men!

Now, here were those disciples, in the same circumstance—fished all night with no catches, and a man tells them to throw their nets down. What do you think went through their minds? (Allow response.) This situation may have seemed familiar to them. The disciples obeyed and caught 153 fish! The disciples recognized the man as Jesus! He had been killed, but was alive again. When they reached the shore, they saw Jesus had prepared fish and bread for them for their breakfast. The Bible tells us this was the third time Jesus appeared to His disciples after He was raised from the dead.

Jesus could have kept His resurrection a secret, but He chose to appear to His disciples. Why do you think He did? Yes, God knew people would have a hard time believing Jesus had been raised from the dead if no one ever saw Him alive again. The disciples were eye-witnesses—they actually saw Him alive again. The disciples told others, who told more people, and through time the event has been retold over and over. There were witnesses who saw Jesus alive after His death. This helps us to know it is true. When we tell others about Jesus' resurrection, we can share with them about times when Jesus appeared to people.

Scripture (Group 3): We've heard how Jesus appeared to His disciples early one morning as He stood on the shore. Group 3 has discovered some other occasions when Jesus appeared to people after He rose from the dead. Have the members of the group take turns sharing a page from the book they created. They can briefly summarize the Scripture verses.

Music (Group 4): Have Group 4 sing the chorus of "He Lives," including the new verse, if they wrote one.

Lord's Supper: As we partake of the Lord's Supper, we are reminded that Jesus gave His life for us. He shed His blood so our sins could be forgiven. Since Jesus rose from the dead, we know that we also can have eternal life with Him. Let's think of these things as we remember Him.

Offering: One way we can thank God for Jesus' resurrection is by the giving of our offerings. Thank You, God, that Jesus is alive and that we can spend eternity with You.

Personal Praise (Group 5): **Group 5 has prepared some skits showing ways we can tell others how Jesus rose from the dead and is alive today.** Have the group present the skits.

Scripture (Group 6): **We know Jesus is alive today because the Bible tells us so. Examples are given where people saw Jesus alive. We know Jesus is alive. He provides our needs and helps us. Group 6 found some verses that tell us various things Jesus does for us today. He could only provide these things for us if He were, indeed, alive.** Have the pupils take turns reading verses. End with group prayer.

Closing Moments
● ● ● ● ● ● ● ● ● ● ● ● ● ● ● ●
(10 minutes)

For this activity have the children cut out fish shapes. They should write on each fish the sentence, "I will tell _____ about Jesus' being alive." Each child can make as many fish as he wishes. Have an area where the fish can be taped in a "pond." Next week the pupils can report how many people they told about Jesus.

Jesus Is Alive!

John 20:10-18

John 20:19, 20

John 20:24-29

Luke 24:13-31

Acts 1:1-11

1 Corinthians 15:3-8

John 21:1-14

Directions: Look up the Scriptures to find out who Jesus appeared to after He arose from the dead.
Draw a simple illustration to go with each Scripture.
Cut apart the boxes on the dotted lines, and staple the pages together to form a book.

Read the situations below. Decide what each boy or girl should do to speak up and tell the truth about Jesus' resurrection.

1
Emily said to Abby, "I can't believe you think Jesus rose from the dead! It's just a story, like a fairy tale. How can you believe it's really true?"

Abby said . . .

2
Jenny and Derek were cousins. They were sad because their great-grandma was very sick. Derek said, "What if Great-grandma doesn't get better? What if she dies? What will happen to her?"

Jenny said . . .

3
Chris and Beth's teacher told them there are many different religions. The teacher said that some people worship Jesus, and other people worship other gods. Beth said to Chris, "It really doesn't matter which god a person chooses to worship. What's the difference between Jesus and any other god?"

Chris said . . .

4
Mark invited Jeff to go with him to a week of church camp. "Do you talk about Jesus there?" Jeff asked. "I don't see what the big deal about Jesus is. He lived and died just like any other man. Why is He so special?"

Mark said . . .

Speak Up
for Jesus

7B

Gifts and Blessings

Jesus is alive. He has, and He will, provide those who believe in Him with blessings and gifts. Read these verses to find out some of the blessings we have from Jesus.

Philippians 4:7

1 John 1:9

Matthew 6:31-33

Philippians 4:19

Romans 15:13

Ephesians 4:7

Jesus Will Return

Worship Focus
• • • • • • • • • • • • • • • •

Worship God because Jesus will return.

Transition Time
• • • • • • • • • • • • • • •
(10 minutes)

Send the children in small groups to the rest room and drinking fountain. Welcome newcomers and involve everyone in the following activity.

Tic-tac-toe: Before the session begins, draw a tic-tac-toe grid on a chalkboard or poster board. Print some words from Acts 1:1-11 on separate index cards. Scramble the letters in the words. Divide the children into two teams—X's and O's. Have a team member from one team choose an index card without seeing the word on it. The leader should write the scrambled word on a chalkboard or poster board. The person has ten seconds to unscramble the word. If he is successful, he gets to put a mark on the tic-tac-toe board. If he cannot do so, a member from the other team gets a chance. Continue back and forth with the two teams until the word is unscrambled. The first team with three marks in a row wins.

Launching the Theme
• • • • • • • • • • • • • • •
(10 minutes)

Have any of you ever had to move to a new city? Did you have to say good-bye to your friends? How did you feel? (Allow time for discussion.) It is hard to say good-bye to people we love. Sometimes our grandparents or cousins may live far away from us, and we only see them a few times a year. It is hard to say good-bye because we know we will miss them.

Imagine how the apostles must have felt when Jesus was killed. Then Jesus came back to life again. How do you think they felt then? (Allow response.) But they had to say good-bye again. Jesus disappeared from them into a cloud. They may have thought He was now gone forever. But two men in white told them Jesus would return. Imagine their joy. Today we are worshiping God because Jesus will return!

Building the Theme
• • • • • • • • • • • • • • •
(30 minutes)

1. **Call to Worship.** For this activity you will need activity page 8A and the words

to verse 5 of the song, "Wounded for Me." If your children did not learn this hymn before, use one more familiar, such as, "How Great Thou Art," "Jesus Is Coming Again," or "One Day!" Use only the verses that deal with Jesus' coming again.

Have the children write a reading following the instructions on the activity page. During *Sharing in Worship* the entire group will respond with the line, "Come, Lord Jesus." After the reading, have Group 1 sing the special music.

Talk about the words to the song and the words from the reading. Work on practicing the song to present as special music.

2. Devotion. This activity could be considered a challenge activity. Have the group write up an interview with Luke, the author of Acts. The interview should explain the events of Acts 1:1-11 so the rest of the group will get a general idea of what is found in these verses. During *Sharing in Worship,* present this as an actual interview, with someone interviewing Luke about these events.

3. Scripture. For this activity you will need a chalkboard and chalk or poster board and marker, paper and pencils. Have these Scriptures written on the chalkboard or a poster board. (Or, if you prefer, you could print them on index cards, one for each child.)
1. Philippians 3:20, 21
2. James 5:8
3. 1 Thessalonians 5:2
4. 1 Thessalonians 4:16-18
5. 2 Peter 3:9, 10
6. Revelation 1:7
7. Revelation 22:12
8. Revelation 22:20

Have the children look up the Scripture verses and write what information there is about Jesus' return.

What can we know for sure about the return of Jesus? (Allow discussion.) **We**

know we should eagerly await His return, our bodies will be made like His, it is near, He will come like a thief in the night, He will come with loud command and trumpets, the dead will rise first, we will meet Him in the air, He will come with the clouds, all will see Him. What do we *not* know about the return of Jesus? (The time or day.)

4. Scripture. For this activity you will need activity page 8B and pencils. Have the children work the puzzle. The remaining letters that were not crossed out in the Word Search will spell out, "Be my witnesses." Choose one pupil to report this message at the beginning of the Lord's Supper meditation.

After the puzzle is completed, focus a discussion on helping the children understand that we have a command to obey while we are here on earth waiting for Jesus' return.

Sometimes it is hard to wait for special days such as birthdays or holidays. Time seems to go very slowly.

A JOB TO DO

Draw a line through the letters spelling words taken from Acts 1:1-11. The remaining letters will tell you the job we are to do while waiting for Jesus' return.

Word List

Theophilus	Jerusalem	wait
Samaria	sky	gift
Jesus	white	two
apostles	power	men
cloud	Judea	hid
Heaven	earth	do
	Galilee	

Our job: B E M Y W I T N E S S E S

Activity Page 8B

It may seem like a long wait while we anticipate the return of Jesus. But we are commanded to be His witnesses while we are waiting. We need to be telling others about Jesus' life, death, and resurrection. We need to tell them Jesus is going to return.

5. Personal Praise. For this activity you will need clay and an area with a table where the clay can be worked. Have the pupils use their imaginations and create something out of the clay to show they believe Jesus is alive and will return. The piece could show their expression of joy about the anticipation of His return. During *Sharing in Worship* they may share what they made and tell how it shows their feelings. The clay pieces may be used to help tell others about Jesus.

How do you feel knowing Jesus is going to return? (Allow response.) **It makes us excited to know He is coming back for us. It makes us feel good to know where we are going to spend eternity. We should want to share this news with others so they, too, have the opportunity to believe Jesus and look forward to His return.**

6. Personal Praise. This activity could be a challenge activity. You will need materials to create puppets, such as Styrofoam balls, pencils or empty paper towel rolls, and markers. Have the group work on writing a puppet show and creating the puppets for it. The show should be about a situation in which someone is telling others that Jesus will return.

What should we be doing while we are waiting for Jesus to return? (Telling others.) **Why is it sometimes hard to tell others about Jesus?** (Allow response.) **Maybe we are afraid people won't believe us or will laugh at us. Acts 1:8 tells us we will have power to tell others. God will help us to tell others about Jesus.**

Sharing in Worship
● ● ● ● ● ● ● ● ● ● ● ● ● ● ● ● ●
(30 minutes)

Omit any of the following sections if you did not offer the corresponding activity.

Call to Worship (Group 1): Have the group do the reading, including the entire group to say, "Come, Lord Jesus." After the completion, have the group sing the song they learned.

Devotion (Group 2): **Group 2 will present an interview with Luke, the author of Acts.** Have the interview presented, then have the devotional talk.

Devotional Talk: We have just heard an imaginary interview with Luke about Jesus' last time on earth. We can imagine how Jesus' followers felt when they saw Him alive again after seeing Him suffer and die. Jesus showed himself to them, and the Bible says He gave many convincing proofs that He was alive. His followers were probably very happy to have Jesus back with them.

One time, Jesus told them not to leave Jerusalem but to wait for the coming of the Holy Spirit. How do you think this made His apostles feel? (Allow response.) **They were probably a bit confused as to what Jesus was talking about. Jesus told them they would receive power and would be witnesses in Jerusalem, Judea, Samaria, and to the ends of the earth. They were to tell everyone about Jesus' life, death, and resurrection. Then He disappeared behind a cloud into the sky. What would you have thought if you were there?** (Allow response.) **Two men in white, probably angels, appeared and asked them why they were standing there staring at the sky. They said Jesus was taken back to Heaven but would return the same way He left.**

This message wasn't just for the apostles. We can also look forward to

the return of Jesus. He hasn't returned yet, so we must continue to wait, just as the apostles did. What are we supposed to do while we are waiting? (Allow response.) **We should be telling people everywhere about Jesus. We are worshiping God today because of Jesus' return, whenever it may be. But we have a job to do while we are waiting!**

Scripture (Group 3): **There are many places in the Bible that tell about the return of Jesus. Group 3 did some research to find out more information.** Have the group share the verses.

Lord's Supper (Group 4): Have a person from Group 4 tell what job they discovered we are supposed to be doing while waiting for Jesus' return. **Jesus died for us. He shed His blood so our sins could be forgiven and we could spend eternity with Him in Heaven. He also gave us a command to be His witnesses while we are here waiting for His return. As we take the Lord's Supper, let us remember what Jesus did for us and think of a person we can witness to about Jesus' return.**

Offering: One way of saying "Thank You" to the Lord for the promise of Jesus' return is to give our offerings to Him. Let's thank God for Jesus' return as we give our offerings to Him.

Personal Praise (Group 5): **Group 5 made clay creations to show their belief and joy that Jesus is alive and will return for us.** Have the group members share their creations and explain them.

Personal Praise (Group 6): **Group 6 will present a puppet show they created about telling others about Jesus.** Have the group do the play. Then close with prayer.

Closing Moments
● ● ● ● ● ● ● ● ● ● ● ● ● ● ● ● ●
(10 minutes)

For this time have the whole group sing songs praising God because Jesus will return. Children can choose favorite songs to sing.

Joyful Praise

Read Psalm 98:4-9. Paraphrase the verses on the lines below.
Then assign the parts indicated and practice the reading as a group.

Solo 1: (verse 4) _____
_____
_____

All: Come, Lord Jesus!

Duet 1: (verse 5) _____
_____
_____

All: Come, Lord Jesus!

Duet 2: (verse 6) _____
_____
_____

All: Come, Lord Jesus!

Solo 2: (verse 7) _____
_____
_____
_____

All: Come, Lord Jesus!

Duet 1: (verse 8) _____
_____
_____
_____

All: Come, Lord Jesus!

Solo 1: (verse 9) _____
_____
_____
_____

All: Come, Lord Jesus!

A Job to Do

Draw a line through the letters spelling words taken from Acts 1:1-11. The remaining letters will tell you the job we are to do while waiting for Jesus' return.

```
B G E T M M Y T W N
I A N H R E T W N E
H L E E E L D O E M
T I V O W A E D U J
R L A P O S T L E S
A E E H P U F T T K
E E H I S R I I I Y
D U O L C E G A H S
J E S U S J E W W S
D I H S A M A R I A
```

Word List

Theophilus	Jerusalem	wait
Samaria	sky	gift
Jesus	white	two
apostles	power	men
cloud	Judea	hid
Heaven	earth	do
	Galilee	

Our job: ___ ___ ___ ___ ___ ___ ___ ___ ___ ___ ___ ___ ___ ___

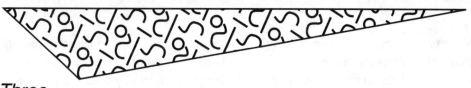

God Cares for Us

Worship Focus

Worship God because He cares for us.

Transition Time

(10-15 minutes)

Pet Show. Before class, ask the pupils to bring pictures of their pets to class. Ask the pupils to tell what they do to care for their pets and the consequences of not caring for their pets. The pupils who do not have pets should tell about a pet they know, or would like to have.

Launching the Theme

(10 minutes)

Pets depend on their owners for everything they need. We also depend on others to care for us. Who cares for you? What do they do? List pupils' answers on the chalkboard. **There is someone who cares for us through our whole lives. He has over five billion people to care for, yet He never forgets**
His job. No one is too small or unimportant for His attention. Who is He? (God.) God cares for each one of you. He knows just what you need, and He gives it to you. In the Bible we learn of a lame man who begged every day for the money he needed to live. Probably many people ignored him and walked by, but God noticed this man. God cared for him by giving Peter and John the power to heal him. We can depend on God to care for us too. Today we'll praise God for caring for us.

Explain choices of *Building the Theme* activities.

Building the Theme

(30 minutes)

1. Call to Worship. Pupils will make flip books. Provide Bibles, copies of activity page 9A, scissors, stapler, and colored pencils. **Read Acts 3:2-8. What did the lame man want? What did Peter and John give him? What did the man do?** God cared for the man by giving him what he truly needed. **Read 1 Peter 5:7. How does God take care of you?** (Gives us parents, teachers, world, health, Jesus.) Even though billions of people live in the world, God cares for (name each pupil). The flip book will remind you that God cares for you. With the colored pencils, color the activity sheet. Write the first letter of your name on the first two pages. Write the letters exactly the same each time. Write the first two letters of your name on pages 3, 4. Write the first three letters of your name on pages 5, 6. Continue until your name is completed on pages 11, 12. (Pupils with more than six letters in their names can add two letters at a time to some pages.) Cut the pages apart on the solid lines. Put them in order and staple at the left side. Flip through the book slowly with your right hand to see the message and pictures "move." During *Sharing in Worship,* this group will demonstrate their flip books and recite 1 Peter 5:7.

2. Scripture. Pupils will portray Bible people. This is a challenge activity. Provide Bibles, pencils, and paper. Before class copy these Scriptures on paper. The answers are in parentheses.

1. Luke 8:22-24 (Disciples; calmed the storm.)
2. Matthew 19:13-15 (Little children; held them.)
3. Luke 9:12-17 (5,000 people; fed them.)
4. Luke 19:2-8 (Zacchaeus; went to his house.)
5. Luke 23:33, 34 (People who crucified Jesus; forgave them.)
6. Acts 3:1-8 (Crippled man; healed him.)

Write on each paper the question, "Whom did Jesus care for?" Write two sentences that tell about that person (people). Write one sentence that tells how Jesus cared for that person (people). For example: I was riding in a boat. I was one of Jesus' twelve helpers. Jesus cared for me by stopping the storm.

Give each pupil one paper. **Read the Scripture and follow the instructions. Choose a verse from your Scriptures that tells how Jesus cared for the person** (people). During *Sharing in Worship,* one pupil will read his three sentences. The large group will guess the person's identity. Then another pupil will read the Bible verse that describes how Jesus cared for the person. Repeat for each Bible person. **Option:** For younger pupils, do the activity as a large group.

3. Devotional. Pupils will make puzzles. Provide Bibles, construction paper, scissors, crayons, and pencils. Write Scriptures and phrases on separate slips of paper. The answers are in parentheses.

1. Psalm 103:3a—have sinned (forgives);
2. Psalm 103:3b—are sick (heals);
3. Psalm 116:6a—are in danger (protects);
4. Psalm 32:8a—don't know what to do (teaches);
5. Deuteronomy 31:8—afraid (never leaves).

If your cat is sick, do you care for it by giving it a bath? No. you give it what it needs—medicine. God cares for us by giving us what we need. Give each pupil one Scripture paper. **You might have one of these problems.** Show the word papers. **Read your verses and select the problem God solves in your verse. On the construction paper write the problem with a crayon. Write how God cares for that person in another color. Then cut the construction paper into three pieces, like a jigsaw puzzle.** For younger pupils, do the activity as a group. During *Sharing in Worship,* pupils will distribute the puzzle pieces among the large group. The pupils will put the puzzles together. As they stand and hold the pieces together, pupils will explain the problem and the way God cares for us.

4. Special Music. Pupils will sing the hymn, "God Will Take Care of You." Provide Bibles, tape player, and cassette tape. Before class tape record the hymn.

What does 1 Peter 5:7 say about God? We should cast our anxieties on God. How do you cast a fishing line? (Throw it.) What are anxieties? Does your Bible use a different word? (worries) Because God cares for us, we can throw all our worries on Him. He'll take care of us. What worries do you have? (Having friends; getting along with family.) God will take care of you. If you or someone you know is familiar with sign language, teach the children how to sign a verse or two of this hymn. Practice several times. During *Sharing in Worship*, this group will sing the song, and sign it if they learned the sign language.

5. Prayer. Pupils will draw pictures. Provide Bibles, black construction paper, and white chalk. **How does God care for us?** (He provides world, answers prayers, helps us.) **Has God cared for you in the ways mentioned in these verses?**

1. Psalm 4:8 (Keeps us safe.)
2. Psalm 16:7 (Teaches us what to do.)
3. Psalm 18:6 (Helps us.)
4. Psalm 25:11 (Forgives us.)

Ask pupils each to draw a picture to show one specific way God cared for him or her. During *Sharing in Worship* pupils will show their pictures and thank God for caring for them.

6. Personal Praise. Pupils will complete a puzzle. Provide Bibles, copies of activity page 9B, and pencils. This activity may be completed without supervision. **How do you think the crippled man felt when he sat begging? How did he feel after he was healed? Our sad feelings turn to joy when we realize that God cares for us.** Complete the activity page by writing the opposites of the clues in the spaces. Write your sentences at the bottom of the page. Share your story with the group. When you are finished, ask your teacher for the answer sheet. Provide a

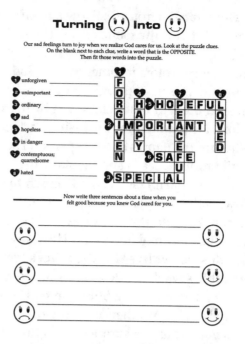

Activity Page 9B

completed activity page. During *Sharing in Worship*, this group will share their personal stories.

Sharing in Worship
(20-25 minutes)

Omit any sections if you did not offer the corresponding activity. The devotional may be given without the group presentation .

Call to Worship (Group 1): **Peter wrote an important verse about God.** Group 1 presents the activity.

Scripture (Group 2): **Let's discover some Bible people God cared for.** Group 2 presents their activity.

Lord's Supper: Read John 3:16. **God showed how much He cared for us by sending Jesus to be our Savior. Jesus showed how much He cared by willingly going to the cross and dying for us. Right now, let's think about Jesus' suffering and death for our sins.** Serve the Lord's Supper.

Devotional (Group 3): Show a fresh flower. **What is the name of this flower?** Tell pupils about the flower—where it grows, what colors it comes in, etc. **God made flowers in a special way. He dressed them in fancy clothes in brilliant colors. He planned for the inside parts. What are the names of these parts?** (The pistil produces seeds and the stamen produces pollen.) **God cares so much for flowers that He planned for them to spread. How do flowers spread?** (The wind, bees, by making seeds.) **How long will this flower live? Maybe a week, yet, the Bible says that a flower has prettier clothes than rich King Solomon had.** Ask a pupil to read Matthew 6:30. **If God takes such good care of a simple flower, won't He take even better care of us? Of course He will.** (Group 3 presents their activity.)

Special Music (Group 4): Group 4 presents their activity.

Prayer (Group 5): **Let's discover how God has cared for us.** Group 5 presents their activity and prays.

Offering: One way to praise God is by caring for others. **Let's share with others in this offering.**

Personal Praise (Group 6): **This group will tell how they feel because God cares for them.** Group 6 shares their activity.

Closing Moments
● ● ● ● ● ● ● ● ● ● ● ● ● ● ● ●
(10-15 minutes)

Charades. Divide pupils into small groups. The groups will take turns pantomiming ways God has cared for them. The other pupils will guess the pantomime. For younger pupils, write suggested pantomimes on slips of paper.

Make a Flip Book

Read 1 Peter 5:7. This flip book will remind you that God cares for you. Color the pages below. On the line, write the first letter of your first name on pages 1 and 2. Write the letters exactly the same each time. Write the first two letters of your name on pages 3 and 4. Keep adding letters of your name one or two at a time until your name is completed on pages 11 and 12. Cut the pages apart on the solid lines. Put them in order and staple at the left side. Flip through the book slowly with your right hand to see the message and pictures "move."

God cares for   1

God cares for   5

God cares for   9

God cares for   2

God cares for   6

God cares for   10

God cares for   3

God cares for   7

God cares for   11

God cares for   4

God cares for   8

God cares for   12

Turning 😟 Into 😊

Our sad feelings turn to joy when we realize God cares for us. Look at the puzzle clues.
On the blank next to each clue, write a word that is the OPPOSITE.
Then fit those words into the puzzle.

1 unforgiven _____

2 unimportant _____

3 ordinary _____

4 sad _____

5 hopeless _____

6 in danger _____

7 contemptuous;
quarrelsome _____

8 hated _____

Now write three sentences about a time when you
felt good because you knew God cared for you.

_____

_____

_____

_____

_____

God's Presence Gives Us Courage

Worship Focus

Worship God because His presence gives us courage.

Transition Time

(10-15 minutes)

Hang-man. Pupils will play "Hang-man." The answers can be single words or phrases. Instruct pupils to think of things they have seen people do that require a lot of courage. Suggestions: walking a tight rope, working on a tall building, talking in front of a large group of people.

Launching the Theme

(10 minutes)

You know many brave people. What gave them their courage? (They trusted their skill, they had good equipment, they practiced.) **When a person has courage, he can face difficult situations. Peter and John faced a difficult situation** when they were arrested for teaching about Jesus. The leaders of the Jews ordered them not to talk about Jesus. Peter and John said, "We must obey God, instead of you." Where did they get their courage? Their only special training was the time they spent with Jesus. That was enough! God's spirit was with them. Because God is with us, we can do courageous things too. Today we will praise God because His presence gives us courage.

Explain choices of *Building the Theme* activities.

Building the Theme

(30 minutes)

1. Call to Worship. Pupils will make a verse maze. Provide Bibles, pencils, markers, and poster board. Before class draw 1½" squares on the poster board. **Have you ever been afraid?** (Pupils share.) **How does it help to remember that God is with you?** (He helps us think clearly. He sends people to help. He helps us make right choices.)

Joshua 1:9 tells that when God is with us we have courage. Start at one side of the poster board. Write this verse, using one square per letter. Start with "Be strong." Change the direction of the letters often, to make a maze. You may go any direction, except diagonally. Don't skip squares between words. Use each square only once. Some squares will be empty. Draw a red square around the first letter of the verse. During *Sharing in Worship* the large group will read the verse by solving the maze.

2. Scripture. Pupils will identify courageous Bible people. Provide Bibles, copies of activity page 10A, crayons, scissors, and pencils. **Optional:** lightweight cardboard. Pupils may do this activity without adult supervision. Provide completed postcards with answers and pictures. **Who is the most courageous Bible person you know? What is courage? Courage is being unafraid to do what is right, even if others are doing wrong. Courage is trusting God. This kind of courage comes from God being with us. On your paper are postcards from Bible people. They forgot to sign their names. Your job is to discover who sent the card and fill in his name. The answers are in the Bible verses.** (1. Solomon; 2. Paul; 3. Joshua; 4. Peter; 5. Peter and John.)

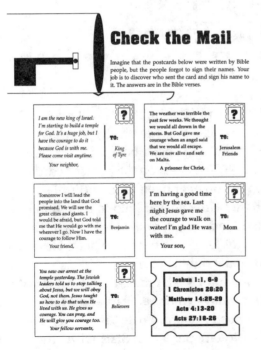

Activity Page 10A

Choose one or two verses from each Scripture telling the courageous thing the person did because God was with him. Now cut out the postcards and draw a picture on the blank side that goes with the story. (Suggestion: for Paul—a ship.) **Optional:** Pupils may copy the postcards (without the answers) onto cardboard pieces. Use these postcards for *Sharing in Worship*. During *Sharing in Worship* this group will read a postcard to the large group. The group will try to identify who sent the postcard. A pupil will read the chosen verse. Continue with the other four postcards.

3. Devotional. Pupils will plan and present skits. Provide Bibles, copies of page 10B, and pencils. This is a challenge activity for older or gifted pupils. **If you wanted to be braver, what would you do?** Write pupils' ideas on paper. Suggestions: take karate lessons, lift weights, make friends with important people. **Read what the Bible says about how to get courage.** Assign these Scriptures:

1. Deuteronomy 31:6
2. 1 Chronicles 28:20
3. Psalm 118:6

What is different about God's courage and the courage that comes from being strong or important? God's courage is real courage. Real courage is being able to choose right. Real courage comes from knowing that God is with us. Read the skit ideas and plan skits about the wrong ways to get courage. In your skits show that other sources of courage don't give real courage to trust God and choose right. During *Sharing in Worship* this group will present their skits then read two of the Bible verses.

4. Personal Praise. Pupils will make an acrostic. Provide Bibles, paper, pencils, cardboard stencils of the letters C-O-U-R-A-G-E, and markers. **When has God**

been with you and given you courage to follow Him? (Pupils share.) Give each pupil one paper and one stencil. **Make a design on your paper by tracing your letter many times. You may color and decorate your letters as you choose.** When pupils have finished the papers, guide them to write an acrostic using the letters. The acrostic sentences will praise God for ways He has given them courage. Begin each sentence with "Because God is with me, I had the courage to . . . " (Suggestion: C—change the TV channel when my friend wanted to watch a bad show.) Each pupil may write the sentence that matches his letter on the back of the paper. During *Sharing in Worship,* the pupils will hold up the papers and say the sentences.

5. Prayer. Pupils will make calendars. Provide Bibles, copies of activity page 10C, crayons, scissors, glue, and paper punch. Photocopy the top of the page on heavy paper; the bottom of the page on regular paper. **When might you be afraid this week? When will you need courage?** (Pupils share.) **Because God is with you, you can have courage. You'll make calendars to remind yourselves that God's presence gives courage. Write in the dates for this week. You'll choose how to complete the spaces by the dates. You can write in the things you'll do that will require courage, or glue one of these pictures or Bible verses in the space, or write your own prayer about courage. Then color the page. Punch a hole in the top, so you can hang your calendar.** During *Sharing in Worship* this group will show their calendars, then ask God for courage for the week.

6. Special Music. Pupils will write words to a song of their choice. Provide tape recorder, blank cassette, Bibles, poster board, and markers. **What is a courageous heart?** (Unafraid, brave.) **Is anyone always brave? No, we are sometimes afraid. Isaiah 43:5a tells us how we can be courageous.** (Pupils read.) **Who gives us courage?** (God does.) **Because God is with us, we can be courageous. Let's write words to a tune you know and like. The words should be about having courage. Think of something or some time that might make you afraid. Then think how you should react when you know that God will give you courage.** As the children suggest words, write them on a chalkboard. Sing the song with the new words, then ask pupils to write the new words on the poster board. If there is time, tape record the children singing their new song. During *Sharing in Worship* the pupils will sing the song or use the tape you have already made.

Sharing in Worship
● ● ● ● ● ● ● ● ● ● ● ● ● ● ● ● ● ●
(20-25 minutes)

Omit any of the following sections if you did not offer the corresponding activity. The devotional may be given without the group presentation.

   Call to Worship (Group 1): **Let's learn the cure for being afraid.** Group 1 presents their maze.

   Scripture. (Group 2): **Many Bible people showed courage because God was with them.** Group 2 presents their activity.

   Lord's Supper: Read Matthew 1:23. **One name for Jesus is Emmanual, which means "God with us." As you eat the Lord's Supper, remember what Jesus was like. That's what God is like too.**

   Offering: Some people don't even know that God wants to be with them and give them courage. The money you give today will help others learn about God.

Devotional (Group 3): **Many people want courage, but try to get it in the wrong places. Group 3 will show us some of these places.** Group 3 presents their skits at this time.

Provide two identical balloons tied onto straws. One balloon should be filled with air, the other with helium. **These balloons look the same. They are the same size and the same color. They are made of the same material and cost the same.** (Cut off the straws.) **Now, that's different! Why did they do that? The insides of the balloons were different. When God is with you, you will act differently. You may not look different, but you will act differently. You may not look different, but you will act with courage. Others will see that God is with you.**

Personal Praise (Group 4): **Let's thank God for the ways He's given us courage.**

Group 4 presents their acrostic.

Prayer (Group 5): **God wants us to act with courage every day. If we remember that He is with us, we can.** Group 5 presents their calendars and prayers.

Special Music. (Group 6): Group 6 sings the song they have written.

Closing Moments

● ● ● ● ● ● ● ● ● ● ● ● ● ●
(10-15 minutes)

The pupils will make buttons from photocopies of the buttons on activity page 10B. (Make copies on heavy paper.) Pupils may cut out a button, staple it to a ribbon, decorate it, and pin it on. **Option:** Pupils may make original designs on name-tag stickers.

Check the Mail

Imagine that the postcards below were written by Bible people, but the people forgot to sign their names. Your job is to discover who sent the card and sign his name to it. The answers are in the Bible verses.

I am the new king of Israel. I'm starting to build a temple for God. It's a huge job, but I have the courage to do it because God is with me. Please come visit anytime.

Your neighbor,

TO:

King of Tyre

The weather was terrible the past few weeks. We thought we would all drown in the storm. But God gave me courage when an angel said that we would all escape. We are now alive and safe on Malta.

A prisoner for Christ,

TO:

Jerusalem Friends

Tomorrow I will lead the people into the land that God promised. We will see the great cities and giants. I would be afraid, but God told me that He would go with me wherever I go. Now I have the courage to follow Him.

Your friend,

TO:

Benjamin

I'm having a good time here by the sea. Last night Jesus gave me the courage to walk on water! I'm glad He was with me.

Your son,

TO:

Mom

You saw our arrest at the temple yesterday. The Jewish leaders told us to stop talking about Jesus, but we will obey God, not them. Jesus taught us how to do that when He lived with us. He gives us courage. You can pray, and He will give you courage too.

Your fellow servants,

TO:

Believers

Joshua 1:1, 6-9

1 Chronicles 28:20

Matthew 14:25-29

Acts 4:13-20

Acts 27:18-26

Looking for Courage
in all the wrong places!

Read what the Bible says about how to get courage: Deuteronomy 31:6; 1 Chronicles 28:20; Psalm 118:6. God's courage is real courage. Read these skit ideas and plan skits about the wrong ways to get courage. In your skits, show that other sources of courage don't give real courage to trust God and choose right. Think about how God's presence could give the kids involved the courage they need.

1 Chad is tired of Butch Bully's teasing. Chad decides to find courage in Al's Weight Room. Guess who he sees at Al's—Butch Bully!

2 Laura is embarrassed to give her speech to the class because she doesn't have a new outfit. She spends all her birthday money on a new outfit, but she still doesn't have the courage to give the speech.

3 Jay doesn't have the courage to say no to his friends when they ask him to do things that are wrong. Jay decides to be best friends with Taylor, because Taylor always does what's right. When Jay's friends show him a bad magazine, Jay looks for Taylor, but Taylor's not there.

4 Martin is afraid that a tornado will hit his home. He saw a plan for a great underground tornado shelter, and knows it will give him courage during storms. The problem? His parents won't build it.

Use these to make badges to wear or to share with others.

I Have Courage

HAVE COURAGE God is here

GOD IS HERE

I am not afraid

Week of _____

Sunday	
Monday	
Tuesday	
Wednesday	
Thursday	
Friday	
Saturday	

Make a Courage Calendar

Because God is with you, you can have courage. Make a calendar to remind you that God's presence gives you courage in whatever you do. Write in the dates for this week. Complete each day's space by noting things you'll be doing and places you'll be going. Glue one of these verses or pictures in each space, or write your own prayer about courage.

"The Lord is the stronghold of my life—of whom shall I be afraid?" Psalm 27:1

"The Lord is with me; I will not be afraid." Psalm 118:6

"When I am afraid, I will trust in you." Psalm 56:3

"Be men of courage; be strong." 1 Corinthians 16:13

"Be strong and courageous. The Lord himself goes with you." Deuteronomy 31:6

School

Sports

Thanks for the courage, God!

Courage in Temptation

Church

Home

10C

God Blesses People Who Give

Worship Focus
• • • • • • • • • • • • • • • • • • •

Worship God because He blesses people who give.

Transition Time
• • • • • • • • • • • • • • • • • • •
(10-15 minutes)

Word Game. Provide Scrabble® letters, large chalkboard and chalk (or sheets of newsprint and pencils). As pupils arrive give each one eight letters. **We'll see how many words our class can make from the letters. As you make a word, write it on the chalkboard (or paper).** You want pupils to discover that they can make more words if they share letters. If they don't learn this on their own, suggest it five minutes before *Launching the Theme*.

Launching the Theme
• • • • • • • • • • • • • • • • • • •
(10 minutes)

Count the words and tell the class the total. **Was it easier to make words when you shared letters? Sure it was. In**

basketball, the best players pass the ball. A player may dribble the ball all the way down the court, yet pass the ball to another player who has a better shot. The reward is winning the game. The Christians in Jerusalem shared everything. The people who had extra money gave it to the apostles, who gave it to the people who didn't have enough. God gave His approval and blessings to these giving Christians. Today we will worship God because He blesses people who give.

Explain the choices of *Building the Theme* activities.

Building the Theme
• • • • • • • • • • • • • • • • • • •
(30 minutes)

1. Call to Worship. Pupils will present a choral reading. Provide Bibles, copies of activity page 11A, and pastel markers. **Name rules about giving. How should you give? Why? How much? To whom? Is there a wrong way or reason to give? Let's read Paul's instructions in 2 Corinthians 9:7, 8, 12, 13. (Pupils read.) The same Scripture is on the activity page. Let's read it together. We'll present a choral reading.** Help pupils decide their lines to read. Alternate between individuals and groups of pupils. Each pupil may highlight his lines with a marker. Practice several times. Again discuss the questions above, this time finding the answers in the Bible passage. During *Sharing in Worship* this group will present the reading.

2. Devotional. Pupils will present interviews. Provide Bibles, paper, and pencils. Older pupils can do this activity without supervision. Before class write these Scriptures on papers:
1. 1 Kings 17:7-16
2. Luke 7:36-38, 48
3. Acts 4:32-37

Write these questions on each paper:
1. Who needed something from you?
2. What did you give?
3. How did God bless you?

We know that God blesses people who give, because He did it in Bible times. Divide pupils into three groups. Give each group a paper. Pupils will read the Scripture and write the answers to the three questions. Each group will choose one pupil to portray the Bible person (answer the questions); the other pupils will be interviewers (ask the questions). During *Sharing in Worship,* each group will present an interview.

3. Scripture. Pupils will demonstrate God's rewards. Provide Bibles, paper, pencils, envelopes, and five used awards of any kind. This is a challenge activity. Before class write these references on papers:
1. Proverbs 28:27
2. Matthew 25:34-40
3. 2 Corinthians 9:7, 8
4. 1 Timothy 6:18, 19
5. Hebrews 13:16

Tell about a time when you were generous. Were you rewarded? How? (Suggest non-material rewards.) **God rewards people who give to others. Take one paper and read the Scripture. Whom did God reward? What was the reward?** Help pupils with difficult concepts. (Answers: gives to poor—lack nothing; feeds, clothes others—Heaven; gives—have all you need; generous—treasures in Heaven; shares—God's pleased.) **For the Scripture you have, write God's reward on the outside of an envelope and on one paper. Attach the paper to one award. Write the person God rewarded on two different papers. Seal one "person paper" in the envelope.** The *Sharing in Worship* presentation will be like the Academy Awards. The pupils will distribute the "people papers" to five pupils in the large group. One pupil from Group 3 will hold an award and tell God's reward. He'll then say, "May I have the envelope, please." Another pupil will bring him the correct envelope. He'll open it and tell the winner of the award. The pupil with that paper will come forward and accept the award. Following each award, a pupil will read the corresponding verse.

4. Prayer. Pupils will write advice letters. Provide Bibles, copies of activity page 11B, and pencils. **Read Acts 4:32-37. Who was Barnabas? What did he do? Today you will be Barnabas. You work for a newspaper. Your assignment is on the activity sheet.**
   Option: With younger students, discuss the letters as a group. They may dictate their answers to you. Suggestions:
1. God gives what we need, not what we want. Your reward was knowing that other people are thanking God for you.
2. I gave because other people needed the money. God rewards me by taking care of me.
3. God met your needs by giving back your coat. You are blessed!
   During *Sharing in Worship* this group will read each letter and a few answers. Then they will pray, thanking God for His blessings when we give.

5. Personal Praise. Pupils will tell how God blessed them when they shared. Provide Bibles, copies of activity page 11C, and coins. **What is God's promise in Proverbs 22:9? When you share, God is pleased and will give you what you need.** Place one activity sheet on the table for every three pupils. Place three books around the sheet to keep the coin from rolling off. A pupil will stand three feet from the sheet and toss a coin onto the page. He will read, "God blessed me when I . . . ," finishing with the section where the coin landed. Then he will share how God blessed him. He must read the Scripture if it lands on that space. Continue until each pupil has had a turn. During *Sharing in Worship* this group will play one round of the game.

6. Special Music. Pupils will make a song rebus. Provide Bibles, a tape recording and copies of "We Are So Blessed," poster board, tape player, and markers. (If you do not have a tape and music of this song, use verse 3 of the hymn, "Count Your Blessings.") Before class draw lines on poster board.

Read Proverbs 22:9. **What happens to a generous man? What is "blessed"?** (Happy; God is pleased.) **When God blesses us, we want to give to others. Then God blesses us more. Let's learn this song.** Sing several times.

Option: After the first "We are so blessed," as the music continues to play, have pupils tell how they've been blessed by God. The pupils will do the same on the second verse, then all sing "When we're empty . . . " to the end. OR write most of the words before class, leaving gaps so pupils can fill in the pictures.

During *Sharing in Worship,* the pupils will teach the song to the large group, using the rebus. If you use "Count Your Blessings," let volunteers tell how they've been blessed after you read through verse 3. Then help them sing the song. After they are familiar with it, have pupils "count their blessings" by listing them on the chalkboard or a poster board.

Sharing in Worship
(20-25 minutes)

Omit any group presentations if you did not offer the corresponding activity. The devotional may be given without the presentation.

Call to Worship (Group 1): **Where can you get everything you need? Group 1 will tell you.** Group 1 presents their reading.

Devotional (Group 2): Before class, write these words with lemon juice on paper: happiness, patience, thankfulness, God's approval. Provide a lamp. **God blessed generous people in Bible times, and He still does today. Let's meet some Bible people.** Group 2 presents their interviews.

Did God give these people everything they wanted? No, God only promises to give us our needs, even though He usually gives much more. Sometimes God gives you rewards that you can see, such as money or food. Often, though, He gives invisible rewards.

When you gave the last cookie to your sister, you may not think you got anything, but God gave you . . . (a pupil holds paper close to hot light bulb until the word appears) **HAPPINESS.**

When you gave the money you were saving for a new cassette to the suffering, God gave you . . . PATIENCE.

When you shared your house with a family whose house burned down, God gave you . . . THANKFULNESS for your home.

When you shared your lunch, God gave you . . . HIS APPROVAL. These rewards are more precious than anything money can buy.

Scripture (Group 3): **And now—the moment we've all been waiting for. We'll learn who won these valuable rewards from God.** Group 3 makes their presentation.

Lord's Supper: Read 2 Corinthians 8:9. **Christ gave up everything in Heaven to come to earth. Think about His great gift today.** Pray and serve the Lord's Supper.

Prayer (Group 4): **Barnabas, a Bible-times Christian, will teach us about God's blessings to people who give.** Group 4 presents their activity and prays.

Personal Praise (Group 5): Group 5 will tell ways they have been blessed.

Special Music (Group 6): Group 6 sings and teaches the song they have learned.

Offering: As the offering is collected, play or sing "We Are So Blessed." If you do not have this, have "Count Your Blessings" taped ahead of time. Close with prayer.

Closing Moments
(10-15 minutes)

Pupils will search newspapers for articles about people who gave to others. They will tell what the person did, and how God might bless him. Suggest non-material blessings too.

Giving

Read the Scripture below, then prepare to present it as a choral reading. The blank spaces next to each line are for indicating who will read that part.

_____ Each one of you should give, then, what he has decided in his heart to give.

_____ He should not give

_____ if it makes him sad. And he should not give

_____ if he thinks he is forced to give.

_____ God loves the person who gives happily.

_____ And God can give you more blessings that you need.

_____ Then you will always have plenty of everything.

_____ You will have enough to give to every good work.

_____ This service that you do helps the needs of God's people.

_____ It is also bringing more and more thanks to God.

_____ The service you do is a proof of your faith.

_____ Many people will praise God

_____ because of it.

_____ They will praise God

_____ because you follow the good news of Christ— the gospel you say you believe.

_____ They will praise God

_____ because you freely share with them and with all others.

2 Corinthians 9:7, 8, 12, 13, International Children's Bible

MEMO

To: Barnabas
From: Editor

Today your assignment is to answer these letters. They are pretty tough.
These Scriptures may help:
Proverbs 22:9
Matthew 6:19, 20
Matthew 25:37-40
2 Corinthians 9:7, 13

Dear Barnabas:
I did what you did. I gave my allowance to a missionary at church. But now I can't go to my school carnival because I'm broke. I didn't get anything from giving. (Well, I did get a thank-you note from the missionary.)
Broke and bored

Dear Barnabas:
I can't understand you. Why did you sell your field and give the money away? You might need it! I think I'll keep what I have.
Holding on tight

Dear Barnabas:
I gave a coat to the downtown mission because I had two. Then I left my coat at the skating rink. The next day it was gone! A week later the manager called. He found my coat under the counter. Was that God's blessing?
A skater

Dear Broke,	Dear Holding,	Dear Skater,

Toss and Share

Put this sheet on the floor or on a table. Stand back three feet and toss a coin onto the sheet. Put books around three sides to keep the coin from rolling off. Take turns saying, "God blessed me when I . . ." and completing the sentence in a way that relates to the space where the coin landed. For example, if the coin lands on the "shared with my family" space, you might say, "God blessed me when I did my sister's chores for her. I felt good because I did a good job, and she was grateful for my help." If the coin lands on the Scripture space, read the Scripture.

Shared something I wanted

Proverbs 22:9

Shared with a person from a different country

Shared with my family

Chocolate Bar

Shared with someone I don't like

Shared with a friend

Shared today

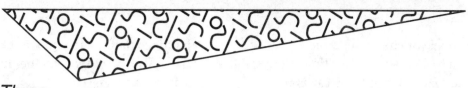

God Knows
Everything About You

Worship Focus

•••••••••••••••••••

Worship God because He knows everything about you.

Transition Time

•••••••••••••••••••
(10-15 minutes)

Getting to Know You. Provide paper, pencils, and shoe box. Ask each pupil to write on a paper one thing about himself or herself that no one in the class knows. (For example: where born, favorite book, a relative's name.) Put all papers in the box. Pupils will take turns drawing a paper, reading it aloud, and guessing who wrote it.

Launching the Theme

•••••••••••••••••••
(10 minutes)

We know each other better now. I've known some of you for years, yet I still don't know everything. Who knows you best? Ananias and Sapphira were believers in Bible times. They sold a piece of land and gave some of the money to the apostles, but they said that they gave all the money. They didn't tell anyone their secret, yet someone knew. Who knew? (God) God punished them for their lie. God knows everything about you. He knows more than even your parents know. He knows you better than you know yourself. That's why we can trust Him to help us do right. Today we will worship God because He knows everything about us.

Explain choices of *Building the Theme* activities.

Building the Theme

•••••••••••••••••••
(30 minutes)

1. Call to Worship. Pupils will make magnets. Provide Bibles, copies of activity page 12A copied on heavy paper, clothespins, scissors, glue, magnetic tape, index cards, pens, and crayons. **Were you ever afraid to tell someone what you did because you thought the person wouldn't like you? God knows everything, and still loves us. These magnets will praise God.** Each pupil will color and cut out one shape from the activity page and glue it on the clothespin. Then the pupil will stick magnetic tape to the back of the clothespin. He or she can clip the clothespin to a verse card. As time allows, pupils may make more verse cards by copying the following verses onto index cards:

1. Psalm 44:21b
2. Psalm 94:11a
3. Psalm 139:1
4. Jeremiah 12:3a

During *Sharing in Worship* this group will show their magnets and read verses.

2. Scripture. Pupils will solve a word puzzle. Provide Bibles, copies of activity page 12B, and pencils. This activity may be completed without adult supervision. Provide a completed activity page. **What things about you can you keep a secret?** (Your thoughts.) **We don't know what you are thinking unless you tell us. Solve this puzzle and learn what the Bible says about your thoughts and secrets.** When pupils are finished, read the verses, match the Scripture texts, and discuss these questions:

1. When are you happy that God knows your thoughts and secrets?
2. When are you afraid?

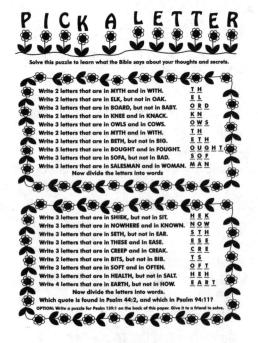

Activity Page 12B

3. What does that make you want to do?

During *Sharing in Worship* the pupils will read the verses.

3. Lord's Supper. Pupils will identify and sort phrases from hymns and Scriptures. This is a challenge activity. Provide Bibles, copies of "Just As I Am," "Amazing Grace," and "How Great Thou Art," blue and red crayons, paper, envelopes, poster board, and scissors. Before class write these verses on papers: Romans 5:8; 1 John 4:9. Divide the poster board into two sections, labeled, "What God Knows About Me" and "What God Feels About Me." Tape one envelope to each half.

Tell about a time when you were on your best behavior. Sometimes we want people to think that we're always polite and well behaved. God knows everything about us—good and bad. (Use only verses 2-5 of "Just As I Am," verses 1, 3 of "Amazing Grace," and verse 3 of "How Great Thou Art.") **In these hymns and Scripture verses, underline with blue pencil all the words that tell what God knows about us. Underline with red pencil all the words that tell how God feels about us, or what He's done for us.** (Example from verse 1 of "Amazing Grace": Blue—wretch, lost, blind; Red—grace, saved, found, see.) Be prepared to explain difficult concepts.

Pupils will copy each underlined word or phrase on a slip of paper. During *Sharing in Worship* they will distribute the papers among the large group. Each pupil will read the word or phrase and decide which category on the poster board describes it. He will put the paper in the correct envelope. Continue for each paper. The pupils from this group will assist as needed. When completed, the pupils should read again the papers from "How God Feels about Us," then pray and serve the Lord's Supper. **Option:** Pupils may sing one of the hymns.

4. Devotional. Pupils will tell what God knew about Bible people. Provide Bibles, black construction paper, white crayons, paper, bright lamp, pencils, and stapler.

Write these references on paper.
1. Genesis 41:15, 16
2. Jonah 1:1-4
3. Matthew 2:3, 7, 13
4. John 13:21-26
5. Acts 5:1-10

Sometimes people are surprised because God knows what they are thinking. Give each pupil/pupil group one paper. **Read the Scripture and tell what God knew about the person.** (Answers: meaning of Pharaoh's dream, where Jonah was, Herod's plan, Judas' plan, Ananias and Sapphira's lie.) Make a silhouette by taping a piece of construction paper on the wall and shining the light toward a pupil's profile. Make five this way. **Cut two copies of each silhouette and staple them together. On the top silhouette, write with white crayon a Bible person's name. On the bottom silhouette, write what God knew about him.** During *Sharing in Worship* the pupils will hold up the silhouettes and tell what God knew about each person.

5. Personal Praise. Pupils will draw a cartoon. Provide Bibles, copies of activity page 12C, and pencils. **Tell about a time when you were treated unfairly because a person didn't know the truth about what happened. God knows everything about us, so He is fair. Look at your activity page. Why are these children happy that God knows everything about them?** (God knows if we're guilty or innocent.) **When were you glad that God knew everything about you and what you did? Draw a picture or write a story about it in the blank space.** During *Sharing in Worship* this group will tell their personal stories.

6. Prayer. Pupils will write prayers. Provide Bibles, paper, and pencils. **In Psalm 139, David praises God because God knows everything about him. Read verses 1-4 and 23, 24. What does God know about David?** Use an *International Children's Bible* to clarify phrases. (God knows schedule, thoughts, ways, words, worries, sins.) Assign each pupil one verse.

Copy your verse on your paper. Then write three sentences telling God why you are glad that your verse is true. (For example, verse 1: Lord, I'm glad you know me because you understand when I get tired of school. You know that it is hard for me to do math. You help me do my best.) During *Sharing in Worship* the pupils will read the Psalm passage as a prayer. Volunteers may read their prayers.

Sharing in Worship
(20-25 minutes)

Omit any of the following sections if you did not offer the corresponding activity. The Lord's Supper and devotional may be given without the group presentations.

Call to Worship (Group 1): Group 1 makes their presentation.

Scripture (Group 2): **Group 2 also learned what God knows about us.** Group 2 reads their verses. **Option:** They may lead the large group in solving a puzzle they worked on.

Lord's Supper (Group 3): **If God knows everything about me, does He still love me? Group 3's activity will answer that question. Option:** Lead the activity as a large group.

Devotional (Group 4): Before class, cut several lips and hands from construction paper. Write across the lips various feelings your pupils may have. (Suggestions: lonely, stupid, afraid, ashamed, happy, thankful.) **Even if you keep a secret from everybody, God still knows.** Group 4 presents their activity.

Stick each lip, with a hand to cover the words, on the wall. **It was good that God knew these people's secrets. God helped Jonah because He knew where he was hiding. Many times we have feelings that we keep secret. Maybe you feel lonely at school because your friends are in the other class. Don't keep it a secret!** (Remove hand from "lonely" lips.) **Tell God how you feel. He knows and will help. Maybe you feel stupid because you failed a test. Don't keep it a secret!** (Remove hand from "stupid" lips.) **Tell God how you feel. He knows and will help.** (Continue for other feelings written on lips.)

Offering: Read Matthew 6:2-4. **God knows how much you will give today. He doesn't want us to brag about our offering. We are giving to Him and He sees it.** Pray and collect the offering.

Personal Praise (Group 5): **Group 5 is happy that God knows all about them.** Group 5 presents their activity.

Prayer (Group 6): **David praised God for His knowledge. Let's listen to David's prayer.** Group 6 presents the prayers they have written.

Closing Moments
(10-15 minutes)

Encourage your pupils to do secret good deeds. Be prepared to offer suggestions. For example: Give or make something for another Sunday school class or send anonymous "Thinking of You" notes. In the remaining time, have the pupils work on their ideas.

Make a Magnet

Color and cut out one of the shapes below, and glue it onto a clothespin.
Stick magnetic tape to the back of the clothespin.
Clip the clothespin to one of the verse cards below.
Make more verse cards by copying these verses on index cards:
Psalm 44:21, Psalm 94:11, Psalm 139:1, Jeremiah 12:3.

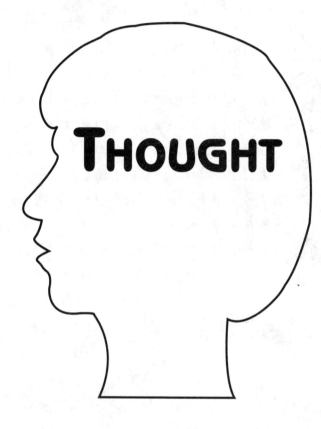

"The Lord knows what is in every person's mind."

1 Chronicles 28:9b,
International Children's Bible

"He understands everything you think."

1 Chronicles 28:9c,
International Children's Bible

12A

PICK A LETTER

Solve this puzzle to learn what the Bible says about your thoughts and secrets.

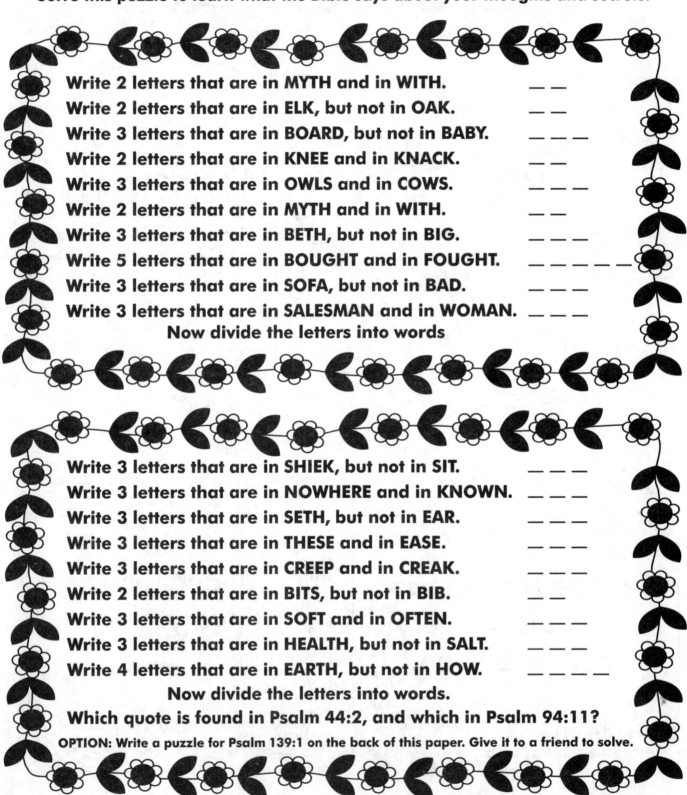

Write 2 letters that are in **MYTH** and in **WITH**.   _ _

Write 2 letters that are in **ELK**, but not in **OAK**.   _ _

Write 3 letters that are in **BOARD**, but not in **BABY**.   _ _ _

Write 2 letters that are in **KNEE** and in **KNACK**.   _ _

Write 3 letters that are in **OWLS** and in **COWS**.   _ _ _

Write 2 letters that are in **MYTH** and in **WITH**.   _ _

Write 3 letters that are in **BETH**, but not in **BIG**.   _ _ _

Write 5 letters that are in **BOUGHT** and in **FOUGHT**.   _ _ _ _ _

Write 3 letters that are in **SOFA**, but not in **BAD**.   _ _ _

Write 3 letters that are in **SALESMAN** and in **WOMAN**.   _ _ _

Now divide the letters into words

Write 3 letters that are in **SHIEK**, but not in **SIT**.   _ _ _

Write 3 letters that are in **NOWHERE** and in **KNOWN**.   _ _ _

Write 3 letters that are in **SETH**, but not in **EAR**.   _ _ _

Write 3 letters that are in **THESE** and in **EASE**.   _ _ _

Write 3 letters that are in **CREEP** and in **CREAK**.   _ _ _

Write 2 letters that are in **BITS**, but not in **BIB**.   _ _

Write 3 letters that are in **SOFT** and in **OFTEN**.   _ _ _

Write 3 letters that are in **HEALTH**, but not in **SALT**.   _ _ _

Write 4 letters that are in **EARTH**, but not in **HOW**.   _ _ _ _

Now divide the letters into words.

Which quote is found in Psalm 44:2, and which in Psalm 94:11?

OPTION: Write a puzzle for Psalm 139:1 on the back of this paper. Give it to a friend to solve.

Who Knows the Truth?

God knows everything about us—but people don't. Sometimes we are treated unfairly because another person doesn't know the truth. Look at the situations below. Why are these kids happy that God knows everything about them?

"My teacher thinks I stole Julie's coin purse. But I didn't! Someone must have put it on my desk to make me look guilty. At least God knows the real truth."

"I didn't mean to break the swing. It was an accident! The recreation director doesn't know how the swing got broken. I could keep quiet, and he'd never know. But God knows. God, please give me the courage to tell the truth."

"'Thanks for cleaning up, Becky. You did a good job, Becky. You're a great babysitter, Becky.' Boy, that makes me mad! Mom and Dad think Becky's so wonderful, but all she did while she was here was watch TV and talk on the phone. I'm the one who cleaned up! God, You know the real truth."

**When were you glad that God knows everything about you?
Draw a picture or write a story about it.**

12C

God Sends People to Teach Us

Worship Focus

Worship God because He sends people to teach us about Him.

Transition Time

(10-15 minutes)

Craft. Before class, ask an adult to teach a quick craft. (For example: pupils write their names in calligraphy, wood burn a small plaque, decorate a cupcake, or tie-dye a handkerchief.) Have all supplies ready, so each pupil can make one item.

Launching the Theme

(10 minutes)

When you have a good teacher, it is easier to learn. Have you ever needed help, but no one would help you? (Suggestions: problem with school assignment, piano lesson, skill in a sport.) **What happened?** (Pupils share.) One day a man was reading the Bible. Read Isaiah 53:7, 8. **"What does this mean?"** he wondered. He needed a teacher. God knew the man's problem and sent him a teacher. God sent Philip to explain the verses and teach the man about Jesus. **How are we like the man?** (Sometimes we don't understand the Bible, or know what to do.) **God sends us teachers too. Today we'll praise God for sending people to teach us about Him.**

Explain choices of *Building the Theme* activities.

1. Call to Worship. Pupils will write paraphrases. Provide Bibles (several versions), index cards, and pencils. This is a challenge activity. **How do you learn about Jesus?** (Pupils share.) **God gave us His Word, the Bible. He also gives us people to help us. Before Jesus went to Heaven, He gave His disciples a job to do. Let's read it.** Read Matthew 28:19, 20. **What was the job?**

Number the phrases of the verses and divide them among the pupils. Each pupil will copy his phrase on a card and number it. Then he will read his phrase from other Bible versions. He will write the same phrase in his own words (a paraphrase) on another card. During *Sharing in Worship* pupils will distribute the cards among the large group. They will find their partners by comparing their cards. They will stand in order according to the numbers on the verse cards. A pupil will read the paraphrases in order, then the verses.

2. Scripture. Pupils will match Bible teachers and pupils. Provide Bibles, copies of activity page 13A, and pencils. **God sent Philip to teach the Ethiopian man. Look at your activity page. The computer at Sacred University erased the students' names on the teachers' class lists. Read the Scriptures given and fill in the names of each teacher's students.** Answers follow:
1. Aquila and Priscilla/Apollos
2. Moses/Israelites
3. Paul/people in Antioch and Lydia
4. Peter/Cornelius
5. Parents/children
6. Lois and Eunice/Timothy

During *Sharing in Worship* this group will read the Scriptures and tell the Bible teacher/student pair.

3. Lord's Supper. Pupils will illustrate book covers. Provide Bibles, paper sacks, crayons, books, and scissors. This activity may be completed without supervision. Furnish two completed book covers. **Who was the best teacher God sent to earth?** (Jesus) **Why was Jesus sent? Read Luke 4:43 for the answer.** (To preach.) **People**

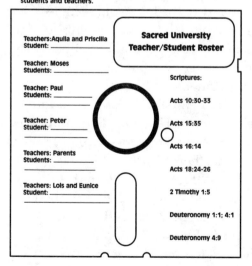

Activity Page 13A

even called Jesus, "Teacher." From these verses, tell what Jesus taught us.**
(Answers are in parentheses.)
1. Matthew 9:11-13 (God loves sinners.)
2. Mark 4:37-39 (God has power.)
3. John 3:16 (God loved us enough to send Jesus.)
4. John 6:1-13 (God cares about the sick, the hungry.)
5. John 13:12-14 (God served us, we should serve others.)

You will make book jackets for these books from paper sacks. (Don't tape to books.) **On your book cover draw a picture and write a title to tell one thing that Jesus taught us about God.** During *Sharing in Worship* this group will explain their book covers, pray, and serve the Lord's Supper.

4. Devotional. Pupils will present a skit. Provide Bibles, copies of activity page 13B, and props. **Option:** If no pupil can ride a skateboard, change the skit to a different skill, such as playing an instrument or rollerblading. **What does David ask God to do in Psalm 25:4, 5?** (Teach him.) **God teaches us in many ways. We have His Word, the Bible. He sent His Son, Jesus. He also gives us people who will teach us. We'll present the skit from the activity page.** Read through the skit, then assign the parts to volunteers. Practice the skit with props, preferably in a private area. Encourage pupils to memorize their lines. During *Sharing in Worship* this group will present the skit.

5. Prayer. Pupils will match countries and missionaries. Provide Bibles, copies of activity page 13C, scissors, index cards, glue, markers (that won't bleed through), and tape. Before class, make a list of missionaries that your church supports and the countries in which they serve. **God not only sends teachers to** (name your city), **but also to far away countries.**

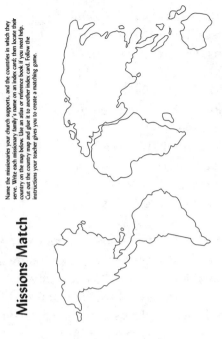

Missions Match

Name the missionaries your church supports, and the countries in which they serve. Write each missionary family's name on an index card; then locate their country on the map below. Use an atlas or reference book if you need help. Cut out the country map and glue it to another index card. Follow the instructions your teacher gives you to create a matching game.

Activity Page 13C

Read Acts 13:2, 3. **What teachers did God and the church send?** (Barnabas and Saul) **Our church helps by giving money to teachers or missionaries.** Name the missionaries and their countries helped by your church. **You'll make a game to match the missionaries with their countries.**

The pupils will write one missionary's name per card. Then they cut out their countries from the map on the activity page. They will glue the countries to cards, one per card. With markers, they will trace around each country and write the name under it. Then they should turn all the cards over, mix them up, and number them. During *Sharing in Worship* they will tape the cards to the wall in numerical order. Anyone from the large group may call out two numbers at a time. A pupil will turn over those cards. If they match a country with the right missionary, remove the cards. If the cards do not match, turn them over and continue the game. When all the cards have been matched, assign each missionary to one pupil, or to a small group of pupils. The pupils will pray,

thanking God for sending their missionaries to teach others about Him.

6. Personal Praise. Pupils will make a mobile. Provide Bibles, heavy colored paper, scissors, markers, string, paper punch, and push pins. Before class cut a 12" circle. Punch holes in it and hang it from the ceiling. **The Ethiopian man was confused about the Bible, but Philip explained it and taught him about Jesus. Even though the two men probably never saw each other after this, what did the Ethiopian man do? Read Acts 8:39.** (He went home rejoicing.) **Who teaches you about Jesus?** (Parents, teachers, ministers, singers, radio personalities, friends, relatives.) **You will cut shapes to represent these people. Then write the name of the person on his or her shape. We'll punch more holes in the circle and tie the shapes to it to make a mobile.** (Ideas: a musical note for Carmen, a radio for Uncle Charlie.) During *Sharing in Worship* pupils will explain the mobile.

Sharing in Worship
(20-25 minutes)

Omit any of the following sections if you did not offer the corresponding activity. The Lord's Supper and Devotional may be presented without the group presentations.

Call to Worship (Group 1): **Before Jesus went to Heaven, He sent out His disciples to be teachers.** Group 1 presents their activity.

Scripture (Group 2): **Group 2 discovered Bible teachers and their pupils.** Group 2 shares their activity.

Lord's Supper (Group 3): **Jesus was the best teacher God sent. Let's learn what He taught us.** Group 3 presents book covers. **Option:** Read the verses from the activity and ask pupils to tell what Jesus taught about God.

Devotional (Group 4): Provide used eyeglasses of different strengths. **Sometimes it's hard to find a teacher. Watch this skit.** Group 4 presents their skit.

Look through these glasses. (Pass glasses around.) **Do they help you see things as they really are? Do they make things look wrong? When glasses are right for you, they help you see. Good teachers are like good glasses. They help you see, that is, *understand* that God loves you, even if you sin. With a good teacher, you can understand that God will protect you. These are true statements about God. Jesus was the perfect teacher. He showed us exactly what God is like. People who teach us aren't perfect, but they help us know God. They are a great gift from God.**

Prayer (Group 5): **Our church helps God send teachers by giving money to missionaries.** Group 5 presents their activity.

Offering: Part of your money goes to help God send teachers. Pray and collect the offering.

Personal Praise (Group 6): **Let's praise God for the people He sent to teach us.** Group 6 presents their mobile.

Closing Moments
● ● ● ● ● ● ● ● ● ● ● ● ● ●
(10-15 minutes)

Name-That-Word Game. Before class, write these words on papers: radio, singer, teacher, grandmother, preacher. Choose four pupils (forming two teams) to play the game. Show a word to one pupil from each team. These pupils will take turns giving one-word clues to their partners. The partners will try to guess the words. When the word is guessed, choose two other pupils to play the game with a new word. If your pupils have difficulty with the words, explain that these words all describe a person or way we can learn about God.

OOPS! DISK-ASTER

Someone accidently erased the disk containing the names of teachers and students. Read the Scriptures below and match the students and teachers.

Teachers:Aquila and Priscilla
Student: _____

Teacher: Moses
Students: _____

Teacher: Paul
Students: _____
_____

Teacher: Peter
Student: _____
_____

Teachers: Parents
Students: _____
_____

Teachers: Lois and Eunice
Student: _____
_____

**Sacred University
Teacher/Student Roster**

Scriptures:

Acts 10:30-33

Acts 15:35

Acts 16:14

Acts 18:24-26

2 Timothy 1:5

Deuteronomy 1:1; 4:1

Deuteronomy 4:9

Assign parts and prepare to present the following skit. You'll need a skateboard with a book taped to the underside, and money.

Bill (walking into store and approaching clerk): I've always wanted to learn to ride a skateboard. Do you think you could teach me?

Clerk: Here's a nice model. (Shows skateboard.) It's great on sidewalks and ramps. All the professionals use it. It's thirty dollars.

Bill: I'll take it! (Hands clerk money, who gives him skateboard). Can you teach me to ride it?

Clerk: I'm sorry. It's time to close. Have fun. (Clerk leaves.)

Bill (talking to himself as he leaves store with skateboard): Maybe this is how you do it. (He sits on the skateboard and pushes with his hands.)

(Jan walks by.)

Bill: Excuse me. Can you teach me to ride this skateboard?

Jan: No, I've never done it, so I don't know how. I think you're supposed to stand up, though. (Walks away.)

Bill: Thanks anyway. (Stands with both feet on skateboard.) This can't be right. It doesn't move.

(Chris walks by.)

Bill: Can you teach me to ride this skateboard?

Chris: Try reading the manual. It's taped under it. (Walks away.)

Bill: OK. (Removes manual. Reads) "Balance your torso so that your center of gravity is directly perpendicular to the vehicle." I can't understand this!

(Carey walks by.)

Bill: Can you teach me to ride this?

Carey: Just watch! (Carey rides the skateboard across the room, then hands it back to Bill.) Nothing to it. (Walks off.)

Bill (calling to Carey as he leaves): Yeah, that's great. But can't you teach ME? Oh, I'll never learn. (Sits on skateboard.)

Tim (approaching Bill): That's no way to ride a skateboard.

Bill: Will you teach me how to ride it?

Tim: Sure. Let's go to my house. I have a huge driveway.

13B

Missions Match

Name the missionaries your church supports, and the countries in which they serve. Write each missionary family's name on an index card; then locate their country on the map below. Use an atlas or reference book if you need help. Cut out the country map and glue it to another index card. Follow the instructions your teacher gives you to create a matching game.

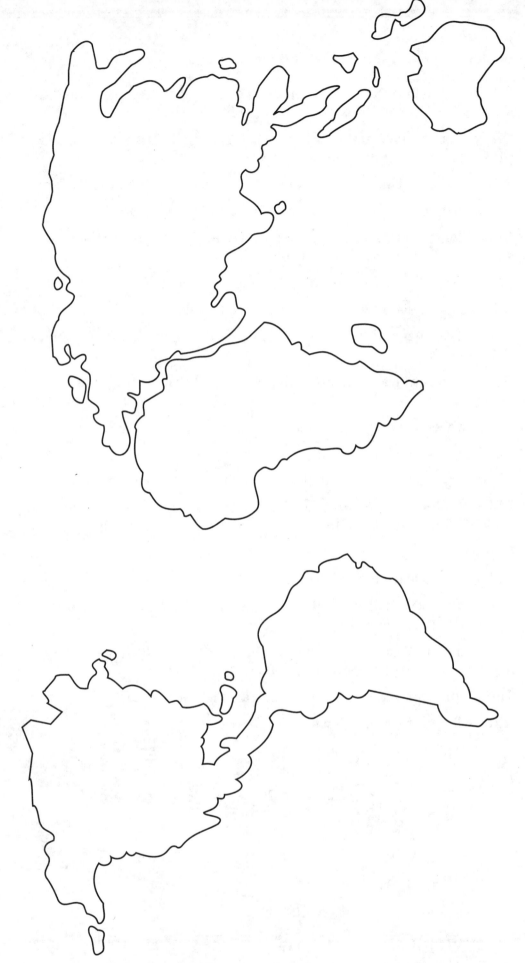